Contents

Copyright 1989
Beacon Hill Press of Kansas City
Kansas City, Missouri

Printed in the United States of America
ISBN: 083-411-2639

Editor
Stephen M. Miller

Editorial Assistant
Kathryn Roblee

Editorial Committee
Stephen M. Miller
Carl Pierce
Dan Riemenschneider
Gene Van Note
Lyle Williams
Aron Willis

Chapter 1

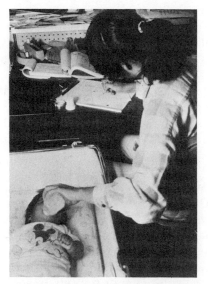

The Working Couple with Children

by Ed and Nancy Robinson

Background Scripture: Ecclesiastes 5:10-20

WE ARE PART of the working couple phenomenon. During the 15 years we have been married, we've spent 12 as a working couple. Ed has been a minister of youth, minister of Christian education, full-time student, and is now a teacher. Nancy has been a teacher's aide, a substitute teacher, and is now a full-time teacher.

Becoming a working couple wasn't our first choice. In fact, it was more like a last resort. It was one of the more difficult decisions of our marriage. We dreamed about living out our ideal: the father at work, the children in school, and the mother at home baking cookies for her happy little family. Alas, this was not to be.

We had no choice. Both of us had to work. One salary wasn't enough for the basic needs of housing, food, clothes, car payments, insurance, and savings for further education. We don't think our story is very different from many.

Reasons to Work or Not to Work

There are some very wrong reasons to become a working couple. One of the worst is so you can keep pace with the life-style of your relatives or friends. Working so you can buy luxuries is hardly worth sacrificing the special bond between the children and the parent who would normally stay home.

Besides, when you're both working you have less time to enjoy the boat or third car or hot tub. In addition, the extra salary may cost you more in taxes, child care, transportation expenses, and aspirin than the second salary is worth.

Another weak reason to become a working couple is to placate your spouse. The decision should never be imposed on one spouse by the other. This decision requires consensus, not a pronouncement by a dictator. There are just too many occasions along the journey of the working couple to say "You made me do this!" or "This is all your fault!"

A third inadequate reason for both parents to work outside the home is to get away from the children. It seems to us that many adults are infatuated with the idea of having a family but are not willing to take the responsibilities that come with parenting. Becoming a parent is a full-time job. If a parent is bored with being home all day with the children, a little creativity in planning outings or volunteering for some church or community services can reduce some of the boredom without paying the price that becoming a working couple demands.

What, then, are some adequate reasons to become a working couple? We feel the only good reason for becoming a working couple is to provide for the needs of the family or the community. The decision to become a working couple should not be one of choice but one of necessity—the necessity of a family who needs more economic resources in order to live, or the necessity of a community that needs the skills of the working couple.

The decision to become or to continue as a working couple should include matters such as when to begin working and how much to work. Sometimes the decision to become a working couple with children can be delayed. While the children are preschool-aged, it is helpful if one parent is home. Such a decision will usually require creative budgeting and delays both in activities and major purchases.

When the children are in elementary school, we have found it important to have one parent home when or shortly after the children get home from school. Such a desire sometimes requires waiting for the right job to come along—one with flexible hours that mesh with school schedules.

When the children reach adolescence, it isn't quite so important for a parent to be around all the time. But jobs that keep the family apart during meals, recreational activities, and times of relaxation can separate the adolescent from parents at a time when the teen most needs the family's influence.

The decision that calls for both parents to work outside the home is never an easy one. The process requires a bit of agony, a lot of discussion, some prioritizing of important family issues and values, and much prayer.

Baby-sitter, Preschool, or Day-care?

One of the most important factors of the decision to become a working couple is that of child care. With the increase in working couples, a glut of child care options has also emerged. These options range from the neighbor lady who takes care of three or four children to the franchised preschool operations capable of caring for scores of children at a time. Some corporations have begun to establish child care centers at the workplace to care for the needs of their employees. Churches have also been quick to join in this endeavor. In addition, several "after school" child care services have sprung up to care for the growing population of "latchkey kids"—children who get out of school before their parents get home from work.

When our children were younger, we selected a young mother close to Nancy's school to baby-sit our children during the workday. She had two children who were about the same ages as our daughters. Even though Nancy cried the first day we left them at the sitter, we had a sense of confidence in the caregiver's abilities to provide love, discipline, and protection for our children while we were at work. When our daughters became a little older, we enrolled them in the preschool of the church we attended. And, yes, Nancy cried the first day we left them there, too.

Choosing a child care situation can be a frustrating experience. Should you choose a home care sitter or a preschool? How can you tell whether the tuition costs are in line with the quality of care? Do the expenses for child care eat up most of the financial gain from the second salary? How can you determine whether the caregivers are qualified to provide the service they promise? These questions (and a host of others) give you a glimpse into the difficulty of selecting a child care situation.

We found ourselves looking for five things when we considered child care.

First, we looked for a sitter or a preschool that shared common values concerning faith, ethics, discipline, and respect for our children. When selecting a child care situation, it is essential to investigate the values of the caregivers.

Don't be afraid to ask probing questions about their perspective of life.

Second, we considered a home care sitter when our children were very young and needed the individualized care that a home with fewer children could provide. As our children matured and grew to enjoy the company of others their own age, a preschool became a viable option.

Third, any child care situation should be able to meet the safety, educational, and social needs of children. That doesn't mean the caregiving has to be highly structured with classes. In fact, some educators feel our society is rushing children into academic life. However, the child care situation should give the children ample opportunities to learn from imagination, play, and interactions with adults and other children in a safe environment. This means the caregivers need to understand how young children develop and learn.

Look for adequate adult caregivers who exhibit genuine love for children, an environment that provides large areas for play, and expressions of creativity through art, building blocks, and the always-favorite playing house, store, or office.

A good way to find out what is happening in the day-care center is to stop by. Most quality day-care institutions will not mind having parents drop by for a visit anytime. Common courtesy suggests that you stop at the administrator's office before you go to the classroom, but a school with a genuine heart for children and a concern for providing quality care usually will not hesitate to encourage parents to visit during the day.

Fourth, most states now require that people who provide regular child care (whether in homes or in preschools) meet some minimal requirements. When our children required child care, we lived in California, which has stringent standards concerning square footage of facilities, educational requirements of caregivers and administrators, student-teacher ratios, and cleanliness and safety of facilities. A license from the local or state authorities does not insure quality care. But it does indicate a measure of accountability on the part of caregivers. It is not improper to ask the potential caregivers for their credentials and references.

Finally, after reviewing credentials and references, take a tour of the facility. Is the home or school clean? Are the rest rooms serviced regularly? Are the rooms in which children play kept free from clutter and dangerous toys? Are adequate sleeping areas provided for each child? Are playgrounds supervised and safe, with sand or some kind of padding under the equipment? Does the home or school prepare meals for the children? Is the meal nutritious? Are the kitchen facilities clean? All of these questions can be answered during a first visit, through a few direct questions and keen observation.

We know of very few parents who leave their children in a child care situation without thinking about them at various times during the day. That kind of concern is natural. On the other hand, if a working parent is preoccupied with concern for their children during the workday because of a lack of confidence in the child care, it may be time to re-evaluate the arrangements. We took time to find arrangements with which both we and our children could be comfortable. We would encourage others to do the same.

Organization at Home

When both parents work, simple chores like grocery shopping, fixing meals, doing laundry, and cleaning the house can become major catastrophes without adequate organization. We are organization nuts. We have labeled boxes in closets, computerized grocery lists, and charts for family chores.

We understand that everyone doesn't have the same organizational fetishes, but some of the things we have discovered might be helpful to you.

Morning can be a terrible time for the working family. Trying to get everyone dressed and fed and out the door on time can be an almost impossible task. We have found that setting the breakfast table the night before can be a real head start toward getting everyone fed. We put out the table setting and all the nonperishable food. In addition, we usually try to pick out the clothes we are going to wear the next day so we don't waste time standing in front of the closet. When our children were younger, we laid out clothes for them. Now they have the responsibility of selecting their own clothes.

Grocery shopping has always been a family affair around our home. When both parents work, there are not a lot of opportunities for the whole family to be together (even going to church doesn't afford such privilege). We decided that shopping for groceries was something we had to do each week, and we would use it as an opportunity for the four of us to be together. It takes a little longer to get through the store keeping track of two daughters and a spouse, but the extra time is worth it since it gets the family together for an hour or so.

Placing the family chores on a weekly schedule and dividing up the responsibilities among the various members of the family can help alleviate the pressure of trying to cram all the housecleaning into Saturday morning or afternoon. Weekends are too short to spend most of the time cleaning house.

One working couple we know with two adolescent children spends two hours every Friday afternoon putting the finishing touches on the housecleaning for the week and then order out for pizza. Doing a little bit of housework each day and splitting up the responsibilities will eventually give you more free time for fun activities.

Very few people we know enjoy doing laundry. Nobody in our home finds the task to be anything other than drudgery. When we used Laundromats we usually combined the task with some other adventure like grocery shopping or lunch at McDonald's. Now that we have our own washer and dryer we find it easiest to do a little laundry every day and not save up several loads for the weekend. By putting a load of laundry in the washer before we go to bed, we can wash and dry it in the morning before we go to work.

Home organization that saves time during evenings and weekends is key. Routine chores that consume all leisure time need to be organized and scheduled to allow for family recreation. Homes have different personalities. Some are super organized and some more spontaneous. But almost every family has to eat, buy groceries, clean house, and do laundry. When you can organize these routine chores into a weekly schedule, it helps you find more recreational time to spend together as a family.

A Collection of Thoughts

In closing, we would like to share with you the condensed version of a few more guidelines we have learned to live by as a working couple with children.

1. When both parents work, it's important that everyone in the family share in the routine responsibilities of the home. That means everyone helps with the cleaning, laundry, bed making, and even cooking and dish washing.

2. Couples need to schedule (that means put specific dates and times on the calendar) to be together as husband and wife. A special night on the town or a weekend away is vital for keeping the romantic flames of marriage alive.

3. Plan special times to be with your children. Help them learn to celebrate the joys of living. Give them quality attention during these times. Don't allow the responsibilities of the workplace to crowd out the responsibility you have to maintain healthy relationships with your children.

4. Don't use the excuse of being a working couple for not being involved in ministry through your local church and to your immediate community. When we are members

of the Body of Christ we are given gifts and abilities to use in ministry. If our work denies us the time or energy to contribute through ministry to others, perhaps we need to reevaluate our job.

5. Our world is flying along at a hectic pace. Most of us working couples have been sucked into the whirlwind. But we need to occasionally fight our way out of that whirlwind so that we can take time to smell the flowers, enjoy quiet moments of reflection about the gracious God who cares for us, and reevaluate the priorities of our faith, family, and life.

Ed Robinson is assistant professor of religious education at Nazarene Theological Seminary in Kansas City. Nancy teaches elementary-age children in public school. Their daughters are 12 and 10.

Chapter 2

Bills, Budgets, and Bank Loans

by Howard Hendricks

Background Scripture: Mark 12:41-44; Luke 12:34; 1 Corinthians 16:2

IT IS CONSERVATIVELY ESTIMATED that 50 percent of the problems of marriage involve finances. Money matters are a major cause of divorce in America.

A cartoon pictured a coed chatting with her soon-to-be-wed friend: "I sure hope you have a happy marriage."

"Oh, we won't have any problems," replied the bride-to-be, "as long as we don't mention money!" She was adding to her marriage vows an invisible exception: "till debt do us part." Debt can be a slowly rising tide that casts an unsuspecting family adrift in a treacherous sea.

No home can escape the clutches of coin and currency. Three aspects of family finances are particularly important: (1) biblical truth concerning money, (2) intelligent management of money, and (3) training of children regarding money.

The Bible is full of examples, exhortations, commands, and warnings about money. Greed is everywhere denounced, and generosity is everywhere extolled. Nor does the Bible contain any apology for its financial emphases.

The Gospels hook the reader on this subject. Jesus Christ said more about money than about heaven and hell combined. Almost every parable relates to finances.

The warp and woof of biblical revelation concerning money is of four main elements.

1. Christian Stewardship Is Total, Not Partial

Everything you possess is sourced in God. It is not what you do with the 10 or 20 percent you give, but rather what you do with the 80 or 90 percent you retain. Many Christians feel that by giving a small percentage they have obviously bypassed all other responsibilities and can do as they please with the remainder. Nothing is further from Scripture.

I think one of the most devastating errors revolves around much of what is taught under the title of tithing. Tithing is presented frequently as if it were something you do in order to get, rather than something you do because of what you have received.

A testimony from a Christian Businessmen's meeting remains vivid: "My business was just about to go under, and I wouldn't have made it. But I decided to tithe. I gave God

10 percent, and from then on my business has been flourishing. Every dollar I give to God, He gives me back two."

That's fantastic! How do you get in on that? I don't know a businessman in America who wouldn't be interested in a deal that guarantees a two-dollar return for every dollar invested. That's good human finances, but that's not good biblical teaching. You give to God whether or not you go broke. You know you never will go broke because you cannot outgive God. James 1:17 declares that every gift originates with God. His major characteristic, James assures us, is His constancy. The only kind of gift He knows how to give is a perfect one.

Paul raises the question in 1 Corinthians 4:7, What do you have that you have not received? Answer: nothing.

2. Giving Is an Investment in Eternity

In 2 Corinthians 9:6 there is a sowing-reaping analogy. If you sow bountifully, you will reap bountifully. If you sow sparingly, you will reap sparingly. The choice in both cases is yours.

Have you ever been caught unprepared in a church or a meeting where they passed the collection plate? You fumble in your pocket or purse. "My shattered nerves! I'm trapped! Nothing less than a five! What a revolting development!" You take the $5.00, and kiss it good-bye.

May I suggest another alternative? Next time the plate goes by, remember that nothing else you have will endure after a period of time. But that money given in faith to God is translated into terms of eternal currency. You need to ask, how is your heavenly stock portfolio? How many eternal securities do you own?

3. Regulate Money
by New Testament Requirements

A pattern is provided in 1 Corinthians 16:2. Giving is to be *regular:* "On the first day of every week." Every time the

Lord's Day arrives you have a reminder of your responsibility in giving.

Giving is to be *personal*. ". . . each one of you should set aside a sum of money."

Giving is to be *systematic*. It is a picture of a little pile, reserved exclusively for Him. It means that God is at the top of the priority list, whether you ever make the rest of the list or not.

Giving is to be *proportionate*. ". . . in keeping with his income." Every time the Lord's Day rolls around, think of the divine prosperity in your life. That becomes the basis. That would transform our giving beyond recognition.

4. Attitude Is Far More Important than Amount

Mark 12:41 says that "Jesus sat down opposite the place where offerings were put and watched the crowd putting their money into the temple treasury." Why such fascination? Because money cuts deeply into character. It's a spiritual barometer, a far more accurate index of your relationship to Jesus Christ than any other element, including prayer, Bible reading, and witnessing. All of these you can do and be shot through with a self-centered spirit. Not so giving —at least not as described here.

"Many rich people threw in large amounts. But a poor widow came and put in two very small copper coins, worth only a fraction of a penny" (Mark 12:41-42). Bless her heart! She didn't give much, but credit her for what she gave—two mites. They make a farthing, a very small amount.

Jesus called His disciples: "I tell you the truth, this poor widow has put *more* into the treasury than all of the others" (v. 43, italics added).

It's perfectly obvious He was not talking about amount; we're already told she gave the smallest denomination. He's talking about attitudes. The scribes cast in out of their superfluity, but she cast in all that she had, even all of her living. If anybody had a legitimate reason for keeping something back, this woman did. She gave it all away, and Jesus Christ said, in effect, "Gentlemen, that is worth observing."

I can still remember from boyhood that my grandmother, who knew Christ as her Savior, often repeated a little verse that sort of dinned its way into my mind:

> *It's not what you'd do with a million,*
> *If a million were your lot;*
> *It's what you're doing at present*
> *With the dollar and a quarter you've got.*

Money Management

Like a volatile gas, money must be managed. It must be contained in a leakproof sack and measured out in proper quantities. It must be directed, applied, and accounted for. This is to say, keep records.

Inadequate records are the primary cause of overspending. Nearly everyone agrees that at least a rough budget must be made, but what happens to the "miscellaneous" section? The mad money? Many homes are shattered on the rocks of financial mismanagement. The key to steering through the channel? Agreement. Who should keep the records? Husband? Wife? The question is not so much *who* as *how*. The one best suited, most inclined toward arithmetic and detail work, should assume the task.

The budget should be determined by need, not wants. The black and white, unemotional facts should be laid out: amount of income, places of distribution, the agreed-upon value system. In our family, for example, we have always leaned toward education in our priorities. We will go without something else in order to buy reading material or pay school tuition. My wife finished her college degree after we had four children. The only way we could work it out was through her attendance at a private university with a substantial tuition rate. We budgeted that tuition because we agreed that her degree was more important at that particular time than a new car, or a bigger house, or nicer, latest style clothes.

Budgets should flow from family prayer, family planning, and periodic evaluation. Christ said, "Where your treasure is, there your heart will be also" (Luke 12:34). We likely would have written it in the reverse: "It's just common sense —where your affections reside, your money will be pressing in close behind." The young lover buys his best girl flowers or jewelry. The sportsman mortgages his income for several years for an imposing boat. But Christ knows the human heart. He asks for an act of the will *first*.

Does it sometimes bother you when you are praying that many Christian enterprises around the world languish while Christians live in luxury? It is not our place to judge our brother who may have a higher standard of living than our own. But it is appropriate to ask, what are we ourselves doing without, in order that the gospel might be spread and believers strengthened?

Of one thing Christians can be sure. God has promised to supply *all* our needs. He who fed 5,000 and turned water into wine for the thirsty wedding guests will provide for us. Sometimes, however, He may also let us suffer lack of resources because of our failure to obey His command to feed the hungry.

Giving develops the giver. That is one reason God ordained that His work be financed by the gifts of His people. Our Lord is not only our Supplier; He is also our Investment Counselor with infallible financial advice. Following Him won't guarantee a healthy dollar profit, but it will guarantee healthy spiritual dividends.

Agree to keep a light hold on money. Fence it in its place. Keep short accounts and assign proper priorities.

Don't believe all the ads. Professional home economists report that the most thorny matters relating to money for young people are rooted in advertising. That is a good word of warning. Stick with your decision once you've made it.

Avoid comparing and coveting. Don't feel sorry for yourself. Face up to the limits of your resources, your anticipated income, and then decide what you can do without. Flee unnecessary luxuries. A money management expert once advised, "Don't try to climb the Himalayas when your income is better suited to the Adirondacks."

List your needs, survey your situation, and draw up a rough budget. Set your major goals by mutual consent. Credit policies? Decide with mutual understanding.

Do a periodic review. When all is said and done, expect the miraculous from God—not from yourself. Be ready to give an account of your financial state. Give generously to those in need, with a willing and a trusting spirit, if God asks you to do it. You cannot force God's provision. Allow Him to teach you the lessons He has for you.

Evangelist Luis Palau tells how he was particularly moved by a crucial need he learned about while traveling. He went home and told his wife that he had pledged $1,000 during the next year for this need. From a missionary's personal budget this was a staggering sum! Together the Palaus prayed and agreed to trust the Lord for the amount. During the year in a most unexpected way, they received a legacy from a family member in that very amount—completely unforeseen! God does seem to have the habit of honoring the faith of the one who steps out in His will.

Training Children to Handle Money

Children soak up parental attitudes toward money like a blotter. You begin very early as a parent to model what they will be doing years later. I remember my father used to ask: "Do you think money grows on trees?" Most children think it grows on Dad and Mom!

The first few nickels and dimes make lasting impressions. Children should have allowances for which they are accountable. There will be casualties.

I remember our daughter Barb desperately wanted to buy cheap, variety store pearls—mostly because the girl next door had some. Against our advice, she spent her entire resources of 25 cents for the pearls. And the very first day she wore them they broke—all over the back of the station wagon coming home from church. That afternoon she crawled upon my lap, lavished me with kisses, and said, "Daddy, I guess I shouldn't have bought the pearls!"

"Really? Why?"

She twisted her face into a disgusted expression.

"Cheap!"

That's bargain tuition—25 cents well invested. We see young people dropping out of school. It's not 25 cents any more, it's more like $2,500. They've never learned how to manage their money.

Don't hesitate to use the law of natural consequences. The child gets his quarter or half-dollar, or whatever, and goes right through it the first day. He has to live the rest of the week without all the other stuff he wants—and maybe needs. You're tempted to bail him out. Don't.

Our son Bob had a paper route. Can you believe it? He threw the paper route for an entire month, and at the end of the month he ended up $64.00 in the hole! I had said repeatedly, as he had ordered his daily draw of papers from the route manager, "Now, Son, you gotta watch that draw!" You see, that's a basic principle.

Encourage a child in a program of work and savings. We have never paid a child in our home for doing chores. I never get paid for mowing the lawn and my wife never gets paid for doing the dishes—and neither does any child. But if my car needs washing, I'll pay, because my time is worth more than the money I invest. If my boy comes and says he needs some extra money and wants to wash my car for me, I say, "Absolutely, Buddy." I am very happy to pay him rather than the man down at the car wash.

Encourage your child to get a job—a paper route, baby-sitting, janitorial work, waiting tables. Did you ever wait tables? That's a liberal arts education. (I don't think you ought to have a license to get married until you've waited tables!) What an exciting experience with humanity—especially with the Christians who come and leave a tract with a dime tip! A job gives a child a chance to save. I believe that you ought to teach a child to save systematically. I have discovered that the child who knows how to manage money is also in the process of learning how to manage time, and every other worthwhile item.

A little boy was given two dimes. He was told one was for the collection plate and the other was for an ice cream cone. He ran down the street and in his enthusiasm he lost a dime down the culvert. Standing there, he looked down and was heard to say, "Well, Lord, there goes Your dime!"

We laugh at that, but that's precisely what many of us are doing—giving God the hot end of the poker.

Reprinted by permission from *Heaven Help the Home!* by Howard G. Hendricks. Published by Victor Books and © 1973 SP Publications, Inc., Wheaton, Ill.

Chapter 3

Untangling the Triangle

by J. Allan Petersen

Background Scripture: Psalm 51:1-7; 1 Corinthians 6:18-20

THE SUSPICION and the discovery of an extramarital affair can be a wrenching emotional experience. Emotions of surprise, shock, anger, fear, hate, and blame come cascading over you like a Niagara. You become confused, and instead of

Editor's Note: Because husbands are much more likely to have an extramarital affair than are wives, this chapter is written to the hurting wife. But the author's words of advice apply also to the husband whose wife has been unfaithful.

your reactions being planned and positive they are unpredictable and explosive.

Sociologist Lewis Yablonsky notes that when an affair is discovered, men are likely to be self-righteous and angry, less likely to see the affair as an act against them, and tend to take action. Women are likely to be hurt; they absorb the news and wonder what's wrong with them, they reexamine the relationship, and tend finally to let the infidelity pass.

It certainly is difficult to think logically and sensibly when your marriage, like a ship, has hit an iceberg and you feel as if everything you've lived for is sinking out of sight. No wonder our reactions are often frantic and impulsive. It is impossible to sit quietly on the tilting deck and map out a strategy for rescue.

However, there is a difference between a ship quickly sinking to the bottom of the ocean and a marriage gashed by an affair. Marriage is a relationship, not an object. Relationships are neither developed nor destroyed in a moment as a result of one experience, good or bad. They grow or deteriorate from many experiences and our reaction to those experiences. Therefore, a panic effort is unnecessary as well as unproductive.

"So your partner has strayed?" asks counselor Evelyn Miller Berger. "That does not mean your life is ruined, that your purpose for living is gone; there is something you can do about it. It may call on your greatest inner resources but even if you fail to save your marriage there yet can be deep meaning to life, and with wisdom and patience you may even save your marriage."[1] An affair is really quite a complex thing and doesn't yield to simple one-shot solutions. It did not begin overnight; it will not be solved overnight. We can and must develop an effective coping strategy because both the injured and the guilty parties are swamped with uncertainties about how to behave.

I have isolated 10 practical principles that will provide us a better understanding of ourselves, the problem, and the solutions. These will help where the affair has just been discovered or where it has been going on for a long time. Even for those not personally affected in any way by an affair at the present time, these principles will be part of an affair-prevention strategy. These are not listed in any order of importance or sequence, but the first four will, I hope, come before the last six.

1. Take Time Before You Take Action

This may be the toughest and most difficult thing to do, but it will certainly be the wisest. To protect yourself from snap judgments and snapping emotions you must back off from the situation instead of rushing into it. "The most important thing to do immediately is nothing," says Dr. Rita R. Rogers, professor of psychiatry at UCLA. "Don't flee into action, but rather retreat into reflection. Evaluate what it all really means to your partner as well as to you."[2]

The tendency upon discovering infidelity is to accuse, blame, threaten, panic. There is no way this kind of approach can be constructive, because you are acting out of your emotions and these can fluctuate wildly when you are suffering the unbearable pain of a breaking heart.

Another suggestion: Don't hurry away on a separate vacation because you "need time to think it through." This only invites more involvement with the "other woman." Maintain your regular routine; keep active physically, keep the house clean, care for the children. Don't give up your responsibilities at home, at church, or in the community, except perhaps for a brief period of rest and relaxation. If you work outside the home, stay on your job. This is important to your healing and self-esteem.

2. Separate the Facts from Your Opinions

When an affair is discovered, the mind of the betrayed goes into high gear. Not only is every kind of emotion experienced, but these emotions are fleshed out in your thoughts day and night. You unconsciously mix the actual facts with your negative opinions of those facts and create a false picture of yourself and of the difficulty.

You must constantly differentiate between what are the real facts and what are negative opinions you have unconsciously mixed with the actual facts. For example: The fact is, "My partner is unfaithful," but you may add a false and negative conclusion: ".'. . therefore he doesn't care for me and the children anymore."

"My husband loves another woman"	—therefore, "I have lost my beauty and am now ugly."
"My partner deceived me."	—"I can never trust him again."
"I've been hurt so deeply."	—"I can never forgive and be healed."
"Our marriage has failed."	—"I'm a failure as a wife and mother."

None of these deductions are valid. The facts are true—the conclusions are false. And because such conclusions are always negative, they destroy your self-esteem and plunge you into hopeless despair.

3. Don't Let the Present Destroy the Past

The distress you are suffering now causes you to wonder if all the marriage and family joys of the past were phony and your partner a hypocrite. There is a tendency to think, "He has always deceived me; he never did love me, didn't mean the things he said." So we lose perspective on the good experiences of the past. The disagreements and difficulties of the past are magnified, exaggerated, and nothing looks good anymore.

Ellen Williams quotes an unnamed wife who wrote after her husband's affair:

We recognized our marriage had been good. This was easier for my husband to affirm than for me. I had a tendency to discount the entire fabric of our years together because of one spot, as though something that had occurred in the present could negate the goodness of the past. We began to recall those years both in the heat of our arguments and in our more quiet times. Our life together had a rich history of shared experiences, three children, and a little grandchild. All of this was put on one side of the scale. It far outweighed the unhappiness of the past year.[3]

So treasure the good times you had—the enjoyment of each other, the laughter, the comfort, the intimacy. Of course, there will be stabs of pain when you think of these things in the light of the present betrayal. But let the positive experiences of the past encourage you to work for a present solution. Don't sacrifice the pleasure of the past to the failure of the present. Don't cancel the past. Cherish it. Build on it.

4. Commit Yourself to Learn—Not to Leave

Discovery of an extramarital affair immediately brings a painful reassessment process. The dynamics between you and your partner will undoubtedly and irrevocably be changed. The relationship will never be the same again. And two questions are always asked, either deliberately or unconsciously, by both the innocent and guilty partner. "Should I leave? Should my partner leave?"

You are ill-prepared to answer those questions in your dazed condition. But you can decide whether for you this tragedy will be the end of a marriage or the beginning of a learning process. After Adam and Eve had disobeyed God and were found out, they immediately blamed God, the devil, each other, and the situation. They chose to blame—not to listen; to lash out—not to learn; to hide—to protect themselves from the disapproval of God and those they loved. People ever since have had the same basic struggle. Dr. Ruth

Neubauer, New York marriage and family therapist, says, "Reconstruction of a marriage depends in large measure on how quickly a couple can move beyond the stages of simply assigning blame. Partners who never move beyond the blaming stage may stay married, but the problems that led to the affair in the first place go unexamined and may result in a cycle of repeated infidelities."[4]

No friend of God or of marriage says an affair is a desirable thing. But an affair is a crisis that pinpoints a need, an indication that a change is necessary—a change-point. One jolted, betrayed wife confessed, "Every time I think of those terrible days, I resolve again to treat my marriage and my husband with more care."

Infidelity is more often a symptom than a cause of marital fracture. Just like the oil light in your car, the flashing light reveals a problem that must be taken care of immediately—a symptom of a major difficulty. The red light does not indicate the car has never been any good, a lemon from the factory. Nor does it indicate the car is ruined and you should call the wrecker. It is a signal, a warning that some important action is necessary.

The affair is an indicator—an alarm, a catalyst for positive change. Determine you are going to learn from it and not use it as a pretext to cop out, give out, or walk out. Even if your efforts are not successful and divorce ensues, you can still learn much that you would not learn any other way. God uses all things—all that we let Him—to teach and to temper us, even the disaster of a fractured marriage.

5. Determine the Facts Before Deciding the Fate

Affairs come in all sizes and shapes and for various reasons.

Though adultery is involved in both a one-night stand and a long-term affair, the dynamics and results vary and each must be handled in a different way. The Bible college dean I counseled who determinedly seduced every girl he could on campus is one thing. A close friend of mine, who, rebounding from a marriage problem, yielded to one experience one night and then confessed it to God and to his wife is another thing.

In his enlightening book *Affair Prevention,* Episcopal minister Peter Kreitler lists eight common types of extramarital affairs: The Friendship Affair, the Be a Good Neighbor Affair, the Cup of Coffee Affair, the Seize the Moment Affair, the Old Acquaintance Never-to-be-forgotten Affair, the People Helper Affair, the Western Affair, and the Office Affair. The names he's given to these tell how or where they begin and are quite self-explanatory, except perhaps the Western Affair. This involves the promiscuous man whose many affairs are like notches on his masculinity belt—as a cowboy might cut notches in his gun stock for every bad guy killed.[5]

You cannot treat a sickness unless you know what kind it is.

Dr. Richard Fisch, professor of psychiatry at Stanford University Medical School, suggests this:

> If you want to repair your marriage instead of dumping your husband, don't try to get him to confess the adultery through questioning, innuendo, or other forms of entrapment. Tell him straight out that you know . . . and how you know. Also wait until the first emotional shock is over before you try to talk about it at all. When at last you do broach the subject, don't use threats, such as divorce or separation, don't keep reminding him that you feel betrayed, that he has forever lost your trust. And don't insist that he go for professional help.[6]

Your only purpose here is to get the facts, not to jump to conclusions or to initiate action.

6. Ask for Reasons, Not for Details

Once you get the honest facts you must explore the reasons for the infidelity—reasons that will help you understand the causes and how you are involved. Why has your husband turned to another woman? What are his struggles? In almost every instance of marital infidelity, the "other woman" is providing something the wife is not giving. Your motive must be to learn and comprehend, not to defend yourself or assign blame—to confront with care, not with criticism—to listen without malice or anger.

This may be the toughest assignment of all—to listen, to put yourself in your partner's shoes, to try to understand his feelings and why he believes the affair took place. Some of the things you hear will be hard to take. They may reflect upon you. You may be hurt, even wrongly accused. One woman told me her husband said, "I can't talk to you, and I just needed someone to talk to." You may feel unjustly criticized. But bite your lip, wipe away the tears, and listen—*listen!* No belittling, no moralizing, no sermons, no Bible verses.

One warning. Do not probe for the juicy details. "Where did you two go when you were together?" "Were you thinking of her when you made love to me?" "Did you ever have her here in our house, in our bed?" One woman, learning her unfaithful husband used the Holiday Inn, exclaimed, "I'll never stay in a Holiday Inn again as long as I live!" There may be some details you are dying to know about, but don't ask them. They are irrelevant to resolving the problem. Knowing them may satisfy your curiosity and fuel your jealousy, but it will not contribute to the solution.

And resist every desire to ask questions that compare you in any way to the other woman, in looks, dress, performance.

Also, please, please don't ask him if he loves you. You force him into a double bind. At this point, he doesn't know; he's torn. He is living in the realm of his feelings and is undoubtedly deceived by those feelings. If you ask, "Do you still love me?" and he tells the truth, he might say, "No," or "I don't know," and then you would be shattered—hopeless.

If he said, "Yes," you would be tempted to believe he is lying or to say, "Then why did you do such a thing? It proves you don't love me." This only aggravates the situation. At this point his actions speak more loudly than anything he can say.

7. Increase Your Growth, Not Your Guilt

Perhaps the hardest thing of all to do—and at the same time the most necessary—is to examine the possibility of your own culpability in the affair.

An unnamed, saddened housewife said: "Looking back, I saw there had been many times—oh, so many times —when my husband reached out for closeness and understanding that I didn't give. I had always been doing something more pressing—like mending, cleaning the refrigerator, or weeding the garden. I recalled the number of times he had said wistfully, 'Why don't we get off by ourselves for a couple of days? You can get a new dress maybe. And we can just loaf and be lazy—and young.' I hadn't said directly, 'Don't be silly; we're grown-ups,' but my lack of enthusiasm had doubtless been obvious."

Upon leaving his Christian wife, an unbelieving husband said candidly, "This girl isn't as pretty as you are—she isn't even very clean about herself. Without me she is an alcoholic. But she is the only person I know who ever needed me and accepted me just as I am. She has something for me you never had."

"From my husband's affair," one woman told me, "I learned so much about myself that I have become an entirely different woman. I faced what I saw and heard about myself and prayed that God would teach me, change me. I had a deep experience with God, was really converted, and my attitudes were changed. Over and over I prayed that God would give me wisdom to become the most perfect mate possible for my husband. Even my husband noticed it."

No marriage is rebuilt unless each partner is willing to

learn from the problem and make positive changes. No direct action on my part will change my partner, but I can change. God's grace is available to make me grow.

8. Allow Each Partner to Own His Own Actions

Since two people make up a marriage, if it fails, both bear some responsibility for its failure. Their responsibility is not alike, but they are alike responsible. One acts, the other reacts; one neglects the partner, the other neglects his vows. One is unfaithful in caring, the other unfaithful in adultery. No one can shoulder the other's burdens. Each must own his own action, regardless of what the other has done. Neither is responsible for the other's actions, but each is responsible for his own behavior.

Shifting responsibility is a well practiced human trait begun by Adam. We like to play the "blame game" and look for a scapegoat.

I remember one man, Carl, who was a master at this. After being with his lover for a day or two he would come home and expect his wife to embrace him and make love with him. When she hesitated or refused he would say, "You are driving me right into the arms of this other woman. It will be your fault if our marriage breaks up. Is this what you want to happen?" He was a con man. The truth was, he had no intention of giving up his affair but wanted to keep the monkey on his wife's back. She was his garbage bag.

Any decision has to shift from blame to responsibility. Just as we *cannot* escape the part we played in the problem, we *dare not* excuse the part others play. We cannot defend the sin of adultery, but at the same time we can acknowledge our sin of neglect that contributed to the crisis. Some rejected wives, out of fear and insecurity, will assume all blame for their husbands' actions and will beg, plead, pressure, and accept any kind of abuse to keep them from leaving. "You can do anything, but don't leave me. What would I ever do without you?" No man in his heart respects that kind of woman. What she may think gives her control over him is really a sign of her weakness. She is saying, "I am not an important person." Her husband will leave her out of lack of respect or continue his affairs and stay to use her as a punching bag or a doormat.

9. Share with a Confidant or a Counselor

According to medical authorities, 80 percent of all problems are self-healing. We should approach marriage problems the same way. "Yes," says Natalie Gittelson, whom I mentioned earlier, "the marriage that knits its own bones, so to speak, often is strengthened in the process. It is only when all else fails and an insoluble emotional emergency exists that psychological help from outside becomes essential."[7] So a couple should go as far as they can in resolving the crisis unassisted by professionals.

However, sometimes the pain of infidelity is so great that the persons involved need to discharge their emotions to someone else before they can begin to be honest with each other. It's very hard to untangle the emotions of anger and guilt and get a fresh perspective. And they need to vent the emotions to someone who won't add fuel to the flames. This should probably be an unbiased third party, a minister, counselor, or family service agency. Forty to 50 percent of all the problems brought to today's minister have to do with marriage and family concerns. To seek needed counseling is a sign of strength, not weakness. It is the same as seeking a specialist's expertise to save your eyesight rather than foolishly and unnecessarily going blind.

Anyone suffering the excruciating pain and loss from an affair also needs a friend, a confidant—one who will listen, but not talk. One who will support, but not sympathize— who will give acceptance but not advice. Everyone has a host of fringe friends who would enjoy sharing juicy morsels of gossip or who always have the right advice for every situation even though their own marriages are hardly vibrant. Avoid these like the plague. Most people do not really understand the complexities or ramifications of an affair and cannot give objective counsel. They are quick to say "what I would do," or "I wouldn't trust him again," or "to thine own self be true." These counselors are a dime a dozen. Don't syndicate your sorrow. Instead, find a sounding board where you can open your heart and calmly express your feelings and let your hair down, a friend who will pray for you or pray with you—one who doesn't have all the answers. A friend, who as the verse says, "will take the chaff and grain together and with a breath of kindness, blow the chaff away."

10. Seek Your Forgiveness, Then Speak Your Forgiveness

As anyone who has been through the experience will testify, restoring a marriage after infidelity is no easy matter. Forgiveness doesn't come quickly. It is costly. But it is the only way to healing and release, the only solution to deep pain.

His forgiveness can be the cornerstone of a stronger-than-ever marriage. Years ago I read a classic story of excellent forgiveness that moves me again as I write it. The woman kept it locked in her heart for half a century but shared it with "Dear Abby" to help others in the same position.

I was 20 and he was 26. We had been married two years and I hadn't dreamed he could be unfaithful. The awful truth was brought home to me when a young widow from a neighboring farm came to tell me she was carrying my husband's child. My world collapsed. I wanted to die. I fought an urge to kill her. And him.

I knew that wasn't the answer. I prayed for strength and guidance. And it came. I knew I had to forgive this man, and I did. I forgave her, too. I calmly told my husband what I had learned and the three of us worked out a solution together. (What a frightened little creature she was!) The baby was born in my home. Everyone thought I had given birth and that my neighbor was "helping me." Actually it was the other way around. But the widow was spared humiliation (she had three other children), and the little boy was raised as my own. He never knew the truth.

Was this divine compensation for my own inability to bear a child? I do not know. I have never mentioned this incident to my husband. It has been a closed chapter in our lives for fifty years. But I've read the love and gratitude in his eyes a thousand times.[8]

---

1. Evelyn Miller Berger, *Triangle: The Betrayed Wife,* 170.

2. Natalie Gittelson, "Infidelity—Can You Forgive and Forget?" *Redbook* (November 1978), 191.

3. Ellen Williams, *Today's Christian Woman* (Winter 1982), 49-51.

4. Susan Jacoby, "After His Affair," *McCall's* (February 1982), 120.

5. Peter Kreitler with Bill Bruns, *Affair Prevention* (New York: Macmillan Publishing Co., 1981), 16-28.

6. Gittelson, "Infidelity," *Redbook,* 191.

7. Ibid.

8. Abigail Van Buren, "When Your Husband Is Unfaithful," *McCall's* (January 1963), 74.

Chapter 4

My Dad Drinks Too Much

by Arthur Hunt

Background Scripture: Mark 11:25; Ephesians 6:1-3;
2 Timothy 1:18-19; 1 Peter 3:15-16

THAT DAY WAS WORSE THAN USUAL. Dad drank beer most of the day, but in between beers he took large quantities of vodka. I usually stayed in my room and avoided him when he drank like that—stayed away from the inevitable conflicts it caused.

I was a 21-year-old college student at the time. Although I'd committed my life to Jesus three years earlier, I still didn't like to be around Dad when he was drunk, and the smell of liquor made me sick. I was thankful that my mom was in Texas visiting relatives; my sister and two of my brothers were gone too. Only 23-year-old Dave was home. Dave had recently returned from an Army assignment in Europe. While he was there, his relationship with Jesus had gotten knocked out of him. He came back incredibly mixed-up and confused.

I was worried because he was home that night. He and Dad had always had an intense love-hate relationship. They both wanted to show love to each other, but they were too much alike—bull-headed and stubborn. Dad made Dave feel like a failure, and Dave had little respect for Dad. No matter what Dad asked him to do, Dave would find a way to disobey. Sometimes I thought they were both like little children.

If one of them would have accepted the other for what he was, they could have had a great love between them, even in the midst of all their problems. They both craved affection.

It was getting late and Dad was hardly able to speak. I had watched him drink for so many years that I knew the stages he passed through. When he'd get drunk on beer he'd just become loud and eventually fall asleep. But vodka put a crazy look in his eyes. He would get mean and everything that came out of his mouth was filthy. I went into the kitchen to get something to drink. I'll never forget the revulsion I felt for my dad as he sat there destroying himself. I knew it was wrong for me to feel that way, and I prayed about it. Somehow God softened my heart, and I sat down and began to talk to the lonely man who was my father.

Everything was fine until Dave came in. I could tell right away that I'd better try to steer the conversation so that he wouldn't get into an argument. Dave was obviously disgusted with Dad. He made one subtle slur and Dad bristled. They began to argue. I tried to calm them down, but the argument gained momentum. Their anger was building, and there was nothing I could do about it.

Dad, caught up in the argument and the booze, lashed out at Dave and said, "You're nothing but a—failure." Then something happened to Dave that I had never seen before. His body tensed and his eyes enlarged. It was as if all the years of being hurt had added up. His hand shot out, knocking the beer and other things off the table. He grabbed Dad, pushed him off his chair and said with absolute bitterness, "I hate you."

I helped Dad up, then tried to get Dave out of the room. But when Dave pushed him, Dad popped too. They were both beyond reason. Dad was yelling at the top of his voice, "No kid of mine is going to hit me in my own house! You'd better get out of here or I'm going to blow your head off!" This made Dave even madder, and he shoved Dad against the wall, telling him he wasn't leaving. He started to walk away and Dad headed for his own bedroom.

"I'll fix you!" Dad yelled.

The Nightmare

I went into Dad's room and found him trying to load his shotgun. He was so drunk he was having a hard time doing it. While I was trying to get the gun away from him, Dave came in and saw the gun.

"You'd shoot your own son?" Dave yelled. And then he came at Dad. He grabbed the gun and they struggled briefly. During the scuffle the shotgun struck the large bedroom windows and smashed them to bits. Glass flew everywhere. Finally Dave got the gun and removed the shells. The two began to wrestle, Dave crying even while he was fighting. As he hit Dad he yelled, "You never loved me, did you? You never loved me!" He repeated it over and over.

Frantically I tried to come between them. When I got them apart Dave told Dad he was leaving the house and not coming back. Dad was furious. As Dave went out the front door to his car, Dad followed him, yelling obscenities. Dave turned around. They met in the middle of the yard, fighting and yelling. I got down with them, still trying to break up the fight, as they rolled around on the wet ground in the dark. But Dave had a 40-pound advantage over me. It was impossible. Finally, after both of them were bleeding and drained of energy, Dad got away and went inside the house. Dave just sat there on the lawn, staring. At last he got up slowly and walked away.

I just stood gazing up at the sky, shaking, crying, and praying. I had prayed for my dad ever since I had become a Christian—for three long years. And there I was, staring up into a dark sky with my lonely prayers unanswered. I had never felt so powerless and empty. And alone.

Close to Home?

Perhaps this scene is all too familiar to you. One or both of your parents drink or maybe your spouse, and, as a result, you suffer—mentally, spiritually, and perhaps even physically. Maybe you've had that same feeling of utter loneliness and despair—the hopelessness that comes from not knowing what to do.

Some of my earliest memories are of my father coming home drunk and arguing with my mother. I always wanted to love Dad, but I grew up hiding from him because of his drinking. When I became a Christian, I had to make a choice. Either I could go on hiding, allowing the bitterness I felt to eat away at me, or I could ask God to change my attitude and help me cope with the father He had given me. God helped me learn to relate to my father. He can help you also, and make your time at home something better than it is now.

The following suggestions are not cure-alls. Each situation is different. My father, for example, always provided for us even in the midst of his problem. And when he wasn't drinking, he was as nice as anyone. Your situation may be more severe or less so, but if you apply some scriptural principles in relating to the parent or spouse who has a drinking problem, you will find that God can work in you to bring about a solution.

Toward a Solution

First, have a clear conscience toward your family member who drinks. Only someone who has had a parent or spouse with a drinking problem knows the bitterness that can grow from being repeatedly hurt. You want to love, but a hate grows in you that seems uncontrollable. You may think the person is not aware of how you feel. You're wrong. He perceives your attitude; you can never hide emotions as strong as disgust and bitterness.

In 1 Timothy 1:18-19 Paul says, "I . . . sent you out to battle for the right armed only with your faith and a clear conscience. Some have laid these simple weapons contemptuously aside and, as far as their faith is concerned, have run their ships on the rocks" (Phillips). Paul is telling Timothy that, next to his faith, a clear conscience is his most essential weapon.

If you have been guilty of bitterness, you need to confess it, first to God and then to the one whom you have offended. Only in this way can you gain a clear conscience.

Assess your attitudes, figure out where you have wronged the person, and ask him for forgiveness. I have found that saying "I'm sorry" is too easy. Instead, say something like: "Dad, I realize I have wronged you by being bitter toward you. Will you forgive me?"

I'll never forget the time I went to my dad, not long after I had become a Christian, and asked him to forgive me for a whole list of things. I picked a time when he wasn't drinking. He was in a good mood, and we were sitting together talking. When I asked him to forgive me, he put his head down trying to hide his tears, and said he forgave me. That was a turning point in our relationship. From then on I could tell him exactly what was on my mind because he knew I was speaking with the right motives. Our honesty grew. Many times after that we sat at the kitchen table and talked.

Your family member may not react like mine. He may yell you out of the room—or shun you in silence. But it's important for you to take the initiative, to clear your own conscience and open the door to response.

Another benefit of asking my dad's forgiveness was that a new kind of love began to develop once I stopped harboring wrong feelings toward him. It was a long process because he was still drinking, still hurting me and other members of my family. But it was a start.

Another reason to gain a clear conscience toward a parent who drinks is the effect on our witness: "In your hearts reverence Christ as Lord. Always be prepared to make a defense to any one who calls you to account for the hope that is in you, yet do it with gentleness and reverence; and keep your conscience clear, so that, when you are abused, those who revile your good behavior in Christ may be put to shame" (1 Peter 3:15-16, RSV).*

If you have wronged your family member, they will feel justified in ignoring your message. If those who drink feel, for example, that you have a spirit of bitterness toward them, you are hurting your Christian witness immeasurably. But if you have cleared your conscience toward them, they will be "ashamed" when they falsely accuse you. The Holy Spirit will have a clearer channel to communicate to them.

Second, forgive from your heart. When I went in and asked my dad to forgive me, I half expected him to say, "No, it's I who should ask *you* to forgive *me*." But he didn't. His eyes were blinded. He didn't know how much he had hurt me through the years. He didn't ask me to forgive him. But I forgave him anyway.

In Mark 11:25, Jesus gives the sobering command, "And whenever you stand praying, forgive, if you have anything against any one; so that your Father also who is heaven may forgive you your trespasses." God expects us to forgive those who wrong us even if they never ask for forgiveness. It's not easy. But it's worth it.

Why is it so hard to forgive? One reason is that withholding forgiveness is a kind of punishment. It's our way of getting back at the one we feel has wronged us. But we must have the mind of Christ. He suffered for us. It wasn't fair for Him to be crucified; He had done nothing. Yet He suffered for you and me because He loved us. Even while He was dying, He forgave the people who were crucifying Him and asked the Father to do the same.

Third, honor your father and mother. It is easy for the children of alcoholics to cop out on this commandment. Ephesians 6:1-3 says: "Children, obey your parents in the Lord, for this is right. 'Honor your father and mother' (this is the first commandment with a promise), 'that it may be well with you and that you may live long on the earth.'"

When a parent has a drinking problem, it is sometimes very hard to give him honor. Remember that the person usually has a very low self-image. There is little self-respect even though the person may *sound* like an egotist. What he needs and wants is to be treated with respect, to be told, "You are important." After I learned this principle, I tried to think of ways to honor my father. Once, when I needed advice on a college matter, I went to him and asked his opinion. His chest swelled. The bond between us grew. I was honoring him. I sincerely wanted his opinion and he appreciated it.

But honoring is not simply buttering up your parents. It is a basic attitude that includes obedience. In the past you may have had so little respect for your parent who drinks that you were unwilling to obey him, or if you did, you were sullen. But God expects us to obey our parents. Having a parent who drinks doesn't change the scriptural principle. (Of course, if your parent asks you to do something that goes against a scriptural principle, God's law has more authority.)

Fourth, keep praying. Pray for your family. Pray that God will make you a peacemaker in the family. Ask Him to make you an example and give you encouragement. Most of all, pray that God will save your family member who drinks. He says in His Word that it is not His will that any should perish, but that *all* should reach repentance. God's will for your parent or spouse is that he will be born again and begin a new life. Never, never give up praying for that.

Frankly, at times when I was praying for my father, I did give up hope. I was praying with little faith. But I *was* praying. Eventually, God supplied the faith.

After that terrible night with Dave, things got worse at our house. My parents separated; Dad drank more and more. I thought things might never change, but I was wrong—God showed me what He could do. Two years after the incident, my dad received Jesus into his life. He was born again.

Like many others, my dad had to sink as low as he could before realizing what bad shape his life was in. He had lost his wife and his job, and he was on a binge when a horrible hallucination scared him enough to let God get through to him. For once he listened, and God came into his life.

After his encounter with God, my dad's drinking problem seemed to disappear. But those of us who love him regret now that he didn't seek treatment and counseling for alcoholism even after he was saved. Without counseling, he has had recurring bouts with the problem. He thought that because he was a Christian, he could take a beer once in a while without being affected. Nothing could have been further from the truth.

I've learned that many who have a genuine rebirth still have a problem with alcohol. The good news is that your family member who drinks will now be more motivated to change. Demonstrating a desire to conquer the problem is the first step in controlling alcoholism once and for all. Urge your parent to see a good Christian counselor as soon as possible after he is saved.

Some of you are still in the midst of a problem with no end in sight. Remember, there is always hope. I prayed for my dad for five years before he was saved. No matter how bad things seem, no matter how much a person drinks, there is hope. Keep praying.

I know it's not easy to live with a parent who drinks. It is difficult to have the right attitude, difficult to love, difficult to forgive. But I've also discovered that God honors our attempts to follow Him—to follow His example of forgiveness and love.

*All Bible references in this chapter are from the *Revised Standard Version,* unless otherwise indicated.

Arthur Hunt is a pastor in Parkdale, Oreg. This chapter was taken from *Your Family,* "My Dad Drinks Too Much," by Arthur Hunt. Copyright 1982 by InterVarsity Christian Fellowship of the U.S.A. and used by permission of Inter-Varsity Press, P.O. Box 1400, Downers Grove, IL 60515.

Chapter 5

Stephen and Linda Miller, with Rebecca and Bradley, two years after Linda's miscarriage.

A Father's Reflections
on a Miscarriage

by Stephen M. Miller

Background Scripture: Exodus 21:22-25; Psalm 139: 13-16

I LEANED CLOSER to the black-and-white image on the television monitor, but I could see no sign of life. The hazy sonogram of our eight-week-old fetus showed no throbbing that would suggest a heartbeat.

"Is this a still picture?" I asked my wife, who is a nurse.

"No," Linda replied, as she continued to study the tiny figure.

The X-ray technician silently moved the scanner over Linda's abdomen to bounce the sound waves off the fetus and capture the shadows on film. Within a few minutes, she produced several photographs for the emergency room doctor.

Hours before I had brushed fear aside. Light bleeding early in pregnancy is common, I had reminded myself. Linda encountered the same problem with Rebecca, our one-year-old.

After the doctor had reviewed the photos and the results of several tests, he came into the treatment room where Linda and I had spent nearly the first half of this Sunday—my 34th birthday.

"Linda," he said. "I'm going to order a couple hormone shots."

Hope surged within me, for surely he wouldn't have done this had the new life already died.

By 2:30 in the afternoon, we were back home. But two hours later Linda began to complain of abdominal cramps. And before long she was gripping her stomach as the pain began to roll in on powerful waves. Thirty seconds of intense inner squeezing would rise to a peak and fall, followed by 30 seconds of relief.

Neither of us admitted it aloud, but we both knew that was labor—the final stages of a miscarriage that would deliver a fetus that could not possibly survive.

Season of Grieving

Linda's doctor said he would meet us back at Emergency, and that he would admit my wife into the hospital.

Our reflex response was to scurry around for some overnight things and to ask our neighbors to watch little Rebecca. But when our minds caught up with our reflexes,

Linda fell into my arms and sobbed. "I didn't want this to happen."

In those moments, I held her and wondered what I could possibly say. Rebecca was sitting at our feet, looking up and smiling curiously as if Mommy and Daddy were teaching her a new game.

"It's OK," I finally whispered.

But it wasn't. For the season of grieving was upon us.

At the hospital, I stood with the doctor in the busy lobby just outside the waiting room doorway. He spoke in a voice that seemed to carry naturally. People all around watched and listened.

"Your wife is in the process of miscarrying. We're getting her ready for a D and C. We'll do it as soon as the surgical team arrives."

I said nothing. From my sad, stone face I looked into his searching eyes.

"You can go into the room with your wife. It will be a few minutes before the others get here."

Linda was lying on an examination bed, waiting for me. "Did he tell you?" she asked.

I nodded. I wanted to say, "I'm so sorry. I love you." But I was engulfed in grief, and knew that the words would only begin before they would dissolve into a sea of emotion. I didn't want Linda leaving for surgery after that. The mourning would wait.

So I sat on a stool at the foot of the bed, and when I did talk, it was about sedate things like blood tests and pain medication. For most of that time, though, I sat quietly as my eyes recorded the images around me.

Patches of veiled red on the sheets that covered my wife.

A three-foot swath of bright crimson, streaking the floor between the bed and a trash container that was overflowing with bloody tissues and opened packages that once held sterile medical supplies.

And on the shelf, beside the sink, a quarter-inch ball of flesh entombed in a clear plastic cup with a snap-on lid.

"The doctor thinks it's part of the gestational sac," Linda said. "He's sending it to pathology."

I looked silently at the cup. And from the raw instincts of life there arose in me an almost overpowering desire to touch the cup and draw it close to me. But I sat motionless. In that instant there was a quiet explosion within, for I knew this was as near as I would ever get to our child. There would be no small, soft body to hold in my arms and mourn over. No baby to bury. No granite stone on which to engrave a name.

When a pair of nurses took Linda to surgery, they directed me to a large and lonely waiting room. There were 8 couches, 18 chairs, 13 end tables, and me. No one but me. A mute television played its scenes, while easy music fell from the ceiling like a gentle evening shower.

These distractions occupied my mind for only a few minutes. Suddenly I was thinking about life in miniature. Little arms and legs, hands and feet, eyes and nose and mouth. Even at eight weeks, the life had all of these.

Maybe I would not have found myself swirling in this torrent of emotion had it not been for my little daughter. Without her, I would not have known all that an eight-week-old life could become. The creation that was dying on a day I should have been celebrating life was just a fetus, an untouchable something I couldn't see or hold, a future event that wasn't yet real or alive.

But as I paced the waiting room and listened to the imagined sounds of a tiny life being drawn into a high-powered vacuum tube the width of a large straw, I thought of a little girl's two-toothed smile. I remembered her hand patting me on the back as I rocked her in the early evening hours. And I remembered her cooing, as she sang herself to sleep.

In the solitude of that room my sad, stone face melted. The life that could have been was gone. All gone. I mourned not only for myself but for a life that would never breathe.

A Healed Helper

Late that night I picked up my sleepy daughter. The neighbors stood on their porch and watched as I began the dark walk home. Once I reached the row of poplars that shielded me from their view, I stopped and buried my head into a tiny shoulder.

The next morning began the condolences. "God knows what He's doing," said several of my Christian friends. I accepted their genuine effort to console me, but in silence I wondered why they thought God was responsible.

Should we blame Him if the egg implanted itself on scar tissue from my wife's previous caesarean section and was unable to draw the nutrients it needed? Would it have been His fault if a carrier of German measles came in contact with Linda and caused fetal damage that induced the miscarriage?

No doubt God could have been directly involved in ending this life. After all, He is God. And no one better than He knows how the pieces of life and death fit together to create the eternal portrait.

But, to me, the heartache of it all seems so out of character for the God I have come to know.

It is in His character to mercifully allow the body to release a life that would have endured but a few painful, surgery-plagued months or years.

And it is in His character to transform those who are hurting emotionally into healed helpers. Three days after Linda returned to the medical-surgical floor on which she works she came face-to-face with the family of a 50-year-old woman who had died two weeks after she was diagnosed as having cancer.

"I appreciate your empathy," the son-in-law told Linda.

"It has really helped." Never before had my wife been told that, even though she had worked 11 years in a hospital. She had grown accustomed to death, but now she had a new awareness of the grief of those left behind.

And it is in God's character to bring about something that happened the night of the miscarriage.

That evening Linda slept the sleep of a medication more powerful than the deadliest grief. But in the early morning hours of a new day, she had a dream. Through a rippling haze, the texture of a reflection in a pond, Linda saw the image of a baby boy. For a moment, the two looked at one another, then Linda whispered the name we would have given our first son. "Jason." And the baby smiled. When Linda reached out to gather him into her arms, he disappeared.

It was as though the dream was God's way of saying the baby is safe and happy.

I believe in an afterlife, not only because of what the Bible says about it, or what science reports about "near death" experiences of people who were brought back to life, but because of an innate sense of immortality within me. I've never been certain, however, about the immortality of the unborn. The Bible isn't clear about this, and modern science has yet to provide the evidence I would like to see. But could there not be, this hour, in the most beautiful garden of heaven, an angel rocking a little boy named Jason? It would be just like God to arrange this.

Perhaps the answer is one we have to trust to creation's First Father.

But there is one thing I know for certain. When Linda told me she could never name another child of ours Jason, I understood why. And in that instant there arose in me, from the center of life where instincts are born, a soothing and healing peace.

Stephen M. Miller is editor of the Dialog Series of books. He and his wife live in Kansas City, and now have two children, Rebecca and Bradley.

Chapter 6

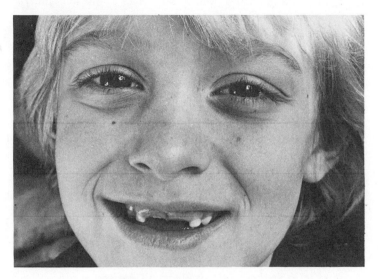

When Your Child
Has a Learning Disability

by Esther Groves

*Background Scripture: Mark 9:33-37; James 1:12;
5:10-11*

THE ONLY YEAR Nathan began public school eagerly
was kindergarten. I walked to school with him the first day:
a handsome five-year-old with dark, curling hair, clear eyes,
and the beautiful golden tan of some Peruvian Indian ances-
tor. He was proud to be going to school and did not hold my

hand until we came up the sidewalk to the kindergarten door. Then he may have felt some of the apprehension, yet also trust, that he showed years before as our newly adopted seven-month-old son.

The kindergarten teacher was smiling. Nathan knew two other classmates—his cousin and a neighborhood girl. He was now a grown-up schoolboy; everything would be all right. And for a short while it was.

But then . . .

What a sinking he must sometimes have felt as he saw the others learning letters and numbers from a puzzling design of black lines and white spaces. How he must have tried at first, believing the teacher when she said that if he tried harder he could see what everyone else saw.

His image of himself must have been damaged as he began to be humiliated by others' misunderstanding. What bravery and courage it must have taken, every year from then on, to go back to that scene of failure day after day.

He began to dawdle on the way to school, sometimes arriving late. Still we did not suspect. Nathan could not tell us what was going wrong, and the teacher said nothing until the end of the year.

There were other signs, but we did not know how to read them. He saw colors differently than we did. He had such good large-muscle coordination that he rode a bicycle the first time he tried, but his poor eye-hand coordination made tying his shoelaces difficult. He was hyperactive, excitable, and impulsive and got into so many things that he reaped many spankings at home and trips to the neighbors to apologize for this and that. At church, while my husband, Carlyle, sat with the choir, I and the children sat in the balcony near the exit to accommodate Nathan's short attention span.

Confidence in ourselves as parents was deteriorating. Carlyle and I became more critical of each other's handling of Nathan. Boys are harder to raise than girls, I thought, remembering our daughter's childhood, smooth even with childhood diseases and accidents.

At the end of the school year the teacher called us in. Our child did not know his letters and numbers, and a psychologist had suggested testing. The tests showed that Nathan had a perception disability caused by an impairment of his nervous system.

Years later, I learned that a child may be quite intelligent and still have such an impairment. Albert Einstein was considered slow as a child, Hans Christian Anderson had trouble learning to read, and Winston Churchill was at the bottom of his class in school. The eye or ear itself may be normal, yet the child sees or hears differently from others because the nervous system is not receiving/storing/sending messages in a standard way—unusual "wiring," you might say.

The psychologist could not tell us with certainty what caused this condition. Nowadays some say heredity may be involved because four times as many boys have it as girls, and it sometimes seems to run in families. Another theory is that if an expectant mother has an inadequate diet—and what could be easier, with our wide choice of junk foods—she may not have enough calcium, magnesium, and certain B vitamins. Then, if during pregnancy she also experiences stress, this makes diet deficiencies surface so that the fetus does not develop as fully in certain ways, and she has one of "those" children: hard to cuddle, hyperactive, with learning disabilities. One government estimate claims that as high as 15 percent of the population has a severe learning disability.

In school, the learning disability shows up in basic skills: reading, writing, spelling, arithmetic, speaking, or listening. Nathan's perceptual difficulty made it hard for him to draw, to keep his place on the page when reading, to remember, to grasp concepts, to read clock time. Another child with different "wiring" might have different problems.

During Nathan's testing, the psychologist rolled up a

sheet of paper, handed it to Nathan, and asked him to look through it. Nathan took it with his right hand and put it up to his left eye. Later the psychologist recommended an eye patch and eye exercise games to strengthen the weak right eye. I bought black cotton and elastic, made two "pirate patches," and put one on Nathan. Suddenly he was very quiet, couldn't cope, had to get out of the house. He and Carlyle went for a walk hand in hand.

"Daddy, I'm frightened."

"What's wrong, son?"

"The cars are upside down."

This was the first time we knew that one eye had been seeing upside down and backward. The eye patch and eye exercises corrected this but not, of course, the nerve impairment.

That fall Nathan returned to kindergarten, and we paid for a tutor who had him trace sandpaper letters and numbers with his fingers so that he would learn them by feel. She had him draw the symbols large—in the air, on the blackboard, on her back—so that he would learn them through movement. In turn she traced them on his back for him to guess. The more of his senses that were involved, the more he learned.

Tutoring helped, but grade school was still not fun. Nathan remembers from then and later: "The words were hard to figure out. Sometimes I couldn't figure them out. They sort of looked alike and ran together. I cried sometimes in school because it was hard. It still is."

A student placed at such a disadvantage may resort to smokescreen stratagems such as clowning in the classroom in order to keep his peers' approval. "What is the capital of Afghanistan?" "Albuquerque?" he said with a big smile to indicate that of course I really know, I'm just hamming it up.

Several years ago, we went to Sierra Leone, West Africa, to work for two years in a literacy program. I ended up teaching Nathan and his young brother, Quentin, at home, since

Nate still needed one-to-one tutoring. At least he didn't have to be compared with others in his grade, and he could progress at his own speed.

I recall one interesting thing: When Nathan read aloud he preferred to sit close by me on the sofa, soaking up emotional support almost by osmosis. I know now he was pushing himself to his limits and needed all the support we could give. Then, change came once again.

Friends in Turpin, Okla., offered Carlyle work there on our return from Africa. I was not all that interested in moving to a new community until a letter came describing the school's new special education program. By the end of the letter I was mentally moving to the panhandle so Nathan could have professional help.

What this help meant was three daily special education classes in basics, designed not for the mentally retarded but for children with learning disabilities. Other subjects Nathan took with the rest of his class. Since he was accompanied by seven other boys in the special education classes, he no longer had continuous one-to-one attention and had to back up and learn to work more on his own. His progress was more solid now: learning was reinforced with special learning materials and equipment, and his comprehension was more thoroughly tested.

This was great as far as it went. The catch is that it goes only through eighth grade.

This year Nathan is an eighth-grader. Next year in all his classes he will have what he now has in only two: textbooks with too-small print in lines too close together, using too-difficult vocabulary to present too-abstract concepts in too much text. What then? Obviously the idea is a high school special education program, but this means hiring another special education teacher and finding an empty room.

The one ray of light is the fairly new law that says schools must provide instruction at the student's level. How this is applied depends on each school and teacher. Parents may request a hearing if the school is not complying with the law.

Last year Nathan took civics with his class. Carlyle recorded textbook chapters on cassette tapes, and the special education teacher used them in classes when the student was supposed to listen to words and follow them with his eye at the same time. However we all concluded that giving too-difficult material twice isn't the same as giving it to the student on his level.

This year we're trying something else. For American history I summarize each chapter in a longish paragraph, underlining the new words a student needs to know. His test over the chapter is the same paragraph, now with blanks for him to fill in, administered at school. This Cloze technique is a method teachers can use when there are no easy-reading texts for a particular course. I learned about it at the last ACLD (Association for Children with Learning Disabilities) national convention. Ideally, the teacher does this, but if the teacher isn't interested I'll gladly offer my help.

There are still ups and down. Nathan said: "One time I got in a fight. The boy called me some bad names and said I couldn't do any work very good, and that I was retarded, so that made me very sad."

He worries about the future: "When I couldn't learn anything I thought I was stupid and dumb, and I thought I couldn't make my way in life, I'd never have a car or anything, I'd always be poor when I grew up." We reassure him that he can do many things (drive on country roads, raise pigs, take complete care of the lawn) and that he is able to learn vocational skills. Every child needs to feel that he is good at *something*.

A person with self-confidence can learn to compensate. I once heard of a young man with a learning disability so severe that he will never read above a second-grade level. He is now straightening fenders and the like in a friend's body shop. When asked how he expected to handle a bank account and checkbook (his mother does it for him now), he laughed and said, "Oh, I'll have my wife take care of that!"

That's the spirit.

Parents can teach their children "survival skills" for living in the world. Perhaps the chief rule is: *don't give up!* Remember Annie Sullivan, in the play *The Miracle Worker* as she tried again and again to teach words to blind and deaf Helen Keller, saying the biggest sin is giving up? If it takes a thousand repetitions to teach something, well then that's what it takes.

But what can parents do who have a child with a learning disability to help that child and make the most of the situation? The ideas that follow are not all mine. Some grow out of our experience as family; others come from workshops I've attended and from reading.

1. Invest in educational toys and games. Let the child see parents having fun putting different kinds of puzzles together and playing games. Hide birthday presents and play "You're hot/cold" as the child looks. Plan treasure hunts and scavenger hunts.

2. Buy socks of all one color if color is a problem. Make charts to show which pants and shirts go together.

3. Make or buy a large cardboard clock face with movable hands and 60-minute spaces around the edge, if telling time is a problem. First practice identifying the hours; later on, half-hours. Then the child learns about minutes, counting how many all together and how many between each number. Next practice counting by fives. A couple of minutes a day on time-telling is better than one too-long session that kills interest.

4. Use rewards for behavior motivation: an M & M or a penny when the child is young, perhaps an accumulation of "tickets" that can be exchanged for something special, like bowling, when the child is older.

Let the child use "crutches" like computers for arithmetic and digital watches for time-telling. What these do is give the child some badly needed self-confidence about being able to master a situation. Don't pressure or overload the child. Above all, be patient, especially when the child forgets things previously learned, or becomes upset and angry.

5. Keep directions simple. Remember that the child sees or hears things differently. Present new concepts in ways the child can see, hear, feel, or touch, if possible. (An example: If a child puts his arms around a globe at its widest part, the equator can be "felt" and understood better.)

6. Give children information on anything they want to know, including sex. Take them to a variety of events so that they know how to behave at each. Practice manners and courtesies. If a child is going to be doing something new, have a "dry run" in advance, maybe a rehearsal at the table for fun.

7. Make responsibilities and privileges go together. Have an "Abuse it, you lose it" rule about privileges. Be consistent with discipline and routines, and put the child in responsible positions. As the child grows up, talk ahead of time about the time he is expected in; don't wait until just when the child is leaving.

8. Make positive suggestions, not negative ones: This can also keep you from saying "no" too often.

9. Teach older children how to use a pay phone, how to use a road map, how to read ads about events, how to keep a checkbook and savings account. Have the kind of information that is usually requested on work applications (birth dates, father's occupation, etc.) typed on a card that the young person can carry and refer to. The older child should also know that if stymied by something on a work application, he can say, "I'd like to take it home and look it over."

10. Look for helpful reference materials to keep on hand at home, such as a low-level easy-reading dictionary and encyclopedia. Easy-reading materials are also available on how to use telephones, read signs, write applications, and so on. Many children may need to carry around with them a card on which an alphabet and a calendar are printed.

11. Don't give up. Children with learning disabilities may not be ready to learn multiplication tables, decimals, fractions, and percentages in fourth or fifth grade, but they should keep on working at them and know them by ninth or tenth. Cutting up paper plates helps to make fractions easier. Other math tricks can also help.

12. Join your school's ACLD chapter, or help to form one if none exists. Your goals might be to:

(1) Help parents exchange experiences and receive information so that they can learn more about their situation, and as a result be more relaxed with, and helpful to, their special children

(2) Educate others by securing special speakers and films, or by preparing programs that can be taken to church or public service groups in the community

(3) Work with your school board in securing special education programs for your school

(4) Help teachers and support them in adapting courses for children with learning disabilities

The greatest support you can give your child is showing daily that you love and respect him for what the child is and for what the child can already do. Your faith in your child is part of your Christian faith.

Esther Groves lives in Turpin, Okla., with her husband Carlyle and their children Debra, Nathan, and Quentin. Esther works as area editor, news reporter, and feature writer for the *Southwest Daily Times,* Liberal, Kans. This chapter was reprinted by permission from *When Your Child . . . ,* by John M. Drescher and others, copyright 1986 by Herald Press, Scottdale, PA 15683.

Chapter 7

When It's Time
to Discipline the Kid

by Howard Hendricks

Background Scripture: Proverbs 13:24; 29:15, 17; Ephesians 6:4

TOO MANY PARENTS assume the role of a Simon Legree. They nail the kid to the floor every time he squeaks; they make a federal case out of every misdemeanor. Others become overly permissive, paralyzed by their child's behavior, scared to death to lay a hand on him for fear of permanently damaging his psyche.

If Junior decides to throw a brick through a plate glass

window, don't stop him. After all, you are likely to curb his genius for pitching.

In the midst of the reality of home life we need an authoritative base for daily disciplinary decisions. Let's examine a slice of scripture that lays a foundation.

Corrective Discipline, Preventative Discipline

The last three chapters of Ephesians are a patrol guide: how to walk by faith when there's a war on. Paul underscores a series of family relationships, and one is the relationship or responsibility of parents to children.

Ephesians 6:4 states: "And, you fathers, stop provoking your children to anger, but bring them up in the chastening and instruction of the Lord" (author's translation).

This does not mean the father is to do all the disciplining, as suggested by, "You just wait till your father comes home!" But the father is *responsible* for all that is done—or not done. The father, as the head of that home, is the one, under God, who will have to give an account of his stewardship.

"Do not exasperate your children" (Ephesians 6:4). This is a very intriguing expression in the original Greek text. It can be translated one of two ways. Either Paul is saying, "Stop provoking your children to anger," or he could be saying, "Don't get the habit of provoking your children to anger." If you're doing it, cut it out. If you're not doing it, don't ever start.

Frequently, people ask, "How does one provoke children to anger?" By either overdisciplining or underdisciplining. Interesting enough, both extremes produce the same result —insecurity.

Children need corrective discipline. Is it essential? Absolutely. Someone asked evangelist Grady Wilson on one occasion, "Did your mother ever spank you?"

"Did she ever spank me? She had a strap in the kitchen which hung under the motto, 'I need thee every hour.'"

That's *corrective* discipline.

Unfortunately, too many parents know only this form of discipline. I was riding in a police car one night when we picked up a kid who had been beaten into unconsciousness by his father. The officer and I counted 67 major welts on this boy's body. When we contacted his father, the first thing he wanted to assure us was that he was a disciplinarian. Truth is, he didn't know anything about discipline. There are too many people running around with a biblical two-by-four who really don't know very much of what the Scriptures teach regarding discipline.

"Cut it out!" "Shut up!" "Stop it!" The kid is seven before he learns his name is not Shut Up. It's amazing how much of this goes on in the name of Christian teaching.

As I've already mentioned, Paul offers a workable option: "Bring them up by *chastening* and *instruction.*"

Every competent physician practices two forms of medicine: corrective and preventive medicine. Every good parent practices two forms of discipline—corrective and preventive discipline. Unfortunately, many of us define discipline only in its corrective aspect.

Corrective discipline is reinforced and made workable by preventive discipline. The effectiveness of corrective discipline is always determined by the relationship you build in preventive discipline. For example, I ask, "Do you play with your child?" If you don't play with him, you have no right to spank him.

Some years ago I was on the grass, wrestling with my son, Bill. We had been dislodged from the living room, where it all began. My wife is unusual—she doesn't appreciate a heated wrestling match in the living room—imagine that. My boy got me in a hold, and I wanted to teach him how to break it. So I pivoted. Unfortunately, I got too much leverage and he went flying through the air like a missile. Oooh! Good night! He's going to have a concussion! They'll try me for child brutality! I cringed inside.

Bill bounced on the unyielding ground, jumped up, and squealed, "Boy, Dad, that was terrific. Do it again."

Now the same child would have dissolved in tears if I had spanked him lightly on the bottom. What's the difference? It's all a matter of relationship—relationships determine response. It's not the physical force but the personal friendship. "The dad who corrects me is also the dad who wrestles with me," concludes the child. Do you fix his bicycle tire or her dollhouse? One message confirms the other. The hardest thing for a child to resist is the displeasure of a parent who has built a strong relationship with him.

Four "Don'ts" on Disciplining

1. Don't use comparisons of one child with another. "Kimberly, why aren't you good like Jennifer?" One intelligent answer: "I'm not Jennifer." (Besides, it's most unbiblical to teach your child to keep his eyes on another person—that can be lethal.)

We are always looking for the parental pharmacist with the patent medicine approach: what are the things you *always* do under *every* circumstance to *always* get guaranteed results? There is no such medicine. This may be one reason God gives most of us more than one child. He wants us to recognize they are individual persons, not products.

2. Don't make fun of a child—especially of his weaknesses. The male of the species is a master with the needle. He may even have practiced before the children were born—on Mom. Coming home from the office, he is heard to bellow, "Well, dear, what's the burnt offering for supper tonight?" That produces a Betty Crocker every time. Sarcasm is like sulfuric acid to human relationships.

I have seen a child with a mild speech problem—occasional stuttering—develop a severe disability because a Ph.D. father and a highly educated mother mimicked their son every time he stuttered. His parents had the dubious distinction of permanently handicapping this young man— and, mind you, he felt called to preach.

It is relatively easy to recognize such failure in its extreme forms. What you may fail to see is what you are doing every day to develop noncorrectable patterns in your own child. Are you on your child's back or on his team?

Be available. Attend the games, the concerts, the science fairs, the drama productions, the PTA. Wear your parent badge with pride. It takes more than words to say: "I am honored to be identified with you." That kind of support enriches the soil in which self-esteem grows best.

3. Don't use idle threats or bribes. I was being entertained in a home where a very bright-eyed grade-schooler was sitting across the dinner table from me. Her mother gave her a helping of mashed potatoes. Then a process unfolded that I have termed "operation rhubarb."

"Sally, eat your mashed potatoes" (in proper parental tone).

"Sally, would you please eat your mashed potatoes for Mommy?" (more plaintive).

"Sally! Eat your mashed potatoes!" (shouting).

"Sally, if you don't eat your mashed potatoes you won't get any dessert" (a soft, slow burn).

I couldn't take my eyes off Sally. She winked at me. Sure enough, soon Mother removed the mashed potatoes, and brought Sally a huge portion of ice cream. I thought, Sally is smarter than her mother. She is a better student of her mother than her mother is of her.

Avoid bribes—they'll get you over a barrel. "Son, if you keep quiet in church today, Daddy will buy you that bat you want." Dad thinks he's solving the problem. Actually, he's creating a greater one. All true discipline has as its goal self-discipline, the development of internal controls.

4. Don't be afraid to say no. Many parents with whom I have counseled confess they were afraid to carry out what they knew was best for the child. I ask, "Afraid? Of what?"

The usual response is, "I feared my child would turn against me, that he would think I didn't love him."

You will seldom lose a child by doing the right thing for him. Intelligent, scriptural love is always unconditional. You may not like what your child does, but you always love him no matter what his response is.

Sometimes, like the surgeon, you have to hurt in order to heal. One of my closest friends is a surgeon. Some time ago I had abdominal pains and went to see him. After checking my X-rays, he said, "You've got a rock collection down there. Since you're not a geologist, Hendricks, we'd better take them out."

"What are the odds?" I asked.

"About 90-10," he said.

"Spell that out," I pressed him.

"About 90 percent you won't live if we don't take them out; about 10 percent you will."

I like a guy who explains clearly. Would you believe it? My choice friend cut me—about eight inches or so. He really sliced me, and he never shed a tear. When he took out the gallstones, he discovered he missed it on the odds by 10 percent. I'd be 100 percent dead by now if my friend hadn't hurt me—because he loved me.

Four "Dos" on Disciplining

1. Project the expectancy of obedience. Some parents never expect their children to obey, and thus they are seldom disappointed.

I had to visit in the home of a 14-year-old delinquent boy once. There was no bell to ring, so I knocked on the screen door and the young fellow responded. He recognized me and invited me to come in and have a seat. Then he said, "I bet you're thirsty, aren't you, Mister." It was a hot day and I was. "I'll go get you some water." He disappeared into the kitchen and came back with a peanut butter jar, not too well washed, filled with water.

Just about the time he got to me, his mother appeared in the door. "Get outa here!" she screamed, and he dumped the whole thing right down the front of me. I have rarely heard a woman—or a man—curse as she did. "That kid can't do anything right!"

"You know, Lady," I replied, "I hate to start this interview on a negative note, but I couldn't disagree with you more. I'm proud of your boy."

"Whad'ya mean, you're proud of him? Look at what he did to you."

"Did you ever make a mistake?" I asked. "To be perfectly honest, if you had shouted at me the way you did at him I'd have spilled that water too."

"He can't do anything right," she repeated again.

"Lady, as long as you continue to say 'he can't,' he won't."

Do you ever tell your child he can't? Telling a child he can't is the basic building block for the shaky structure of inferiority feelings.

2. Don't be afraid to admit your mistakes. I arrived home around eight o'clock one night after a long day of teaching at the seminary. As I walked in the front door, I encountered a clear case of attempted homicide. My two boys were at it again. So I moved into action and disciplined the older boy (obviously the aggressor). As I went into the bedroom my lovely wife said, "Sweetheart, you missed."

"How's that?"

"Let me tell you what happened *before* you arrived."

Of course, her explanation completely changed the picture, and I had to do what I think is very difficult for any parent—apologize. I went out to the kitchen where the older boy, still sobbing, had been assigned to the dishpan. I said, "Bob, I'm very sorry; I acted too soon; I goofed. I didn't have all the facts." I'll never forget his putting his arm around me and saying, "Sure, Dad, that's OK. We all make mistakes."

Your child does not expect you to be a perfect parent, but he does expect you to be an honest one—secure enough to say, "I made a mistake."

3. Allow the child to express his own viewpoint. My students asked me to make a tape of one of our family councils when the children were quite small. We happened to be discussing the problem of tidiness. I realize this is not a hassle for most of you, but there are times when our house seems to resemble tornado alley.

In the course of the discussion, my children were all confessing the sins of their sister, Beverly, who at the time was about four years old.

Little Bev jarred the symposium with a broadside: "But, Daddy, you didn't lower it."

Do you know what she was talking about? Do you have closets in your home? Check out how high the clothes rod is—especially in terms of a four-year-old. I had promised, "Honey, one of these days Daddy will lower it so you can hang up your clothes." But I had not done so.

You see, we were expecting a child of four to do something that was absolutely impossible for her to do.

4. Remember that discipline is a long-range process.

When my wife and I were married we were given a lovely set of pottery. In time our children arrived and we faced a critical decision. Will we keep the dishes intact and have children who do not know how to wash and dry dishes? Or will we train the children to do the dishes, and perhaps in the process lose a few? If you want to know which route we took, you should see the one remaining remnant in our china closet.

Allow your children the luxury of a few mistakes. There is something worse—not making mistakes and arresting growth. Maturity comes with responsibility.

When I was a boy, I loved to play checkers. In fact, I fashioned myself to be something of a champion checker player. There was an elderly gentleman in the community who was purported to be the best, but in my naivete, I felt the reason he had that reputation was that he had never played me.

One day I was hanging around when the action was not too heavy where he played. To my surprise, he said, "Son, how would you like to play checkers?" Before he finished getting the words out I was busy setting up the checkers on the board.

We exchanged a few moves, and then he fed me a checker and said, "Jump me." And then another, and another. I thought, "This is easier than I expected."

As if it were yesterday I can still remember the wry smile that broke out on his lips as I watched him take a checker and move through my men to the other side—"King me." Would you believe, he wiped every checker I had off the board with one king, and I got a liberal arts education concerning playing checkers. No good checker player minds losing a few checkers—as long as he's headed for king territory.

Did you, as a parent, lose a few checkers this week? The question is, where are you headed? King territory? Do you see your child as a problem or a potential? Do you see him in terms of what he is or in terms of what he is to become by the power of God working in him—and in you?

Reprinted by permission from *Heaven Help the Home!* by Howard G. Hendricks. Published by Victor Books and © 1973 SP Publications, Wheaton, Ill.

Chapter 8

The Rebel of the Clan
and Unconditional Love

by Margie M. Lewis

Background Scripture: 1 Corinthians 13; Ephesians 3:17-19

THE FARRONES preferred to stay near home on holidays to avoid heavy traffic. So they spent a beautiful Labor Day afternoon playing golf at their club and ended the day with a picnic supper for the family—the whole family except Tony.

As their celebration ended and Carol Farrone quietly cleared the paper plates off the picnic table, her mind turned to her son. That was the way it always was; she could push aside the thoughts for only a little while before the worries began to haunt her again. Now another holiday had passed with no word.

Preparing for bed later that evening, Carol voiced her concern to her husband, Joe. "It would surely be great if Tony would call."

Joe patted his wife's arm. "It would be nice to at least know where he is."

Joe was taking a shower when the phone rang. Carol picked up the receiver to hear an operator say, "I have a collect call from Tony Farrone. Will you accept charges?"

Before Carol could finish saying she would be glad to accept the call, a weak voice on the other end of the line broke in. "Hi, Mom."

"It's wonderful to hear your voice, honey. Where are you?" Carol asked.

As Tony answered, his feeble words began to fade. "I'm so sick, Mom, and so hungry. I'm really hurting. Tell me what to do."

Carol strained to try to catch her son's last words. Then a strong, businesslike voice boomed into her ear, "Ma'am, your son came dragging into my lobby here a few minutes ago and begged me to let him use our phone to call you. He is in bad shape and he is here at the Holiday Inn." The man named a city 150 miles from the Farrones' home.

"You don't know how much I appreciate your kindness, sir," Carol told the man on the phone. "May I ask one more favor? If you could just put him up in a room I promise we'll be there first thing in the morning to pick him up and pay you for the room and your trouble."

But before the man could respond, Joe Farrone picked up an extension phone and interrupted. "Sir, we'll leave immediately to come and get him. He needs us now. Please keep him there for us."

Within 10 minutes the entire Farrone family piled into their car and took off. (When the two teenage girls learned

Tony had called they wanted to go, too.) The 3-hour drive was a long haul after a tiring day, but an overwhelming feeling of relief rejuvenated them.

They knew without being told that Tony was on drugs again. But at least they finally knew where he was. And that knowledge gave them glad release from the torturous anxiety. It was far easier to deal with the reality of the drugs than the chronic uncertainty and suspense of the preceding months.

The Farrones pulled to a stop as close as they could get to the entrance of the Holiday Inn. As they entered and approached the desk, they spotted Tony across the lobby, sprawled on a couch, obviously strung out. Carol and Joe rushed to their son's side. "We're here, dear," Carol whispered. "It's Mom and Dad. We're going to take you home."

It was minutes before Tony rose close enough to consciousness to realize who was talking. A corpse couldn't have looked more lifeless. His dirt-caked, matted hair hung across his sticky face. His ragged, sweat-soaked clothes were covered with filth from long days on the road. He had worn holes in the soles of both shoes.

Joe went to the desk to settle with the night manager and thank him for the call. The man's pity was penetrating. Joe could read the expression on his face as clearly as if the man had said, "You poor people. You're so different from what I expected. You're not scum at all."

After Tony's numerous fruitless attempts to pull himself up, the Farrones realized their son couldn't make it to the car by himself. So Carol, Joe, and the two girls gently and lovingly shared his weight as they carried him out of the lobby and across the parking lot in the stillness of the early morning hours.

After his father had strapped him into the front seat, Tony slumped to his side and sank into unconsciousness. His father placed a loving arm on Tony's shoulder and tenderly said, "You're having a rough time of it, aren't you, son?"

Tony stirred. But there was no response.

Joe hadn't driven a block before the stench of their son got to the Farrones. The perspiration of days and maybe weeks of hitchhiking together with the vomit of recent hours was more than they could bear. They had to cover their noses and open the car windows for ventilation.

"I remember thinking as I drove home," Joe said. "I've heard so many sermons about the prodigal son in a stinking pigpen. Now here I am holding my nose and living out that very scene. But what really hit me was how thankful the prodigal's father must have felt.

"And then the thought: My son. I love him because he is my son. He has come back home and that's all that matters now."

Once home, the loving thankfulness turned to loving care. The family physician warned that Tony's dehydration had to be corrected immediately; getting liquids into his body was crucial.

So for three days Carol and Joe Farrone gently force-fed their son as if he were a helpless baby. They held open his mouth and dropped in the juices. Finally Tony regained enough strength to care for his own basic personal needs. But it took a month of tender loving care to bring him back to the place where he could function once more on his own.

This experience of the Farrones so vividly illustrates what I feel is the most powerful resource hurting Christian parents can use. That resource is unconditional love.

Parental love can be powerful: It is instinctive up to a point. But unconditional love is even more powerful; and it is not instinctive. In fact, it is unnatural. Unconditional love is the kind of love the Farrones showed that Labor Day evening when they got the call for help from the strung-out son. Theirs was a love without reservation or prerequisites. It demanded no reciprocation, no reward—not even a response.

In researching for this project, I have come across numerous miracles worked through the unconditional love of hurting parents. And in every case the parents shared at least one thing in common with the Farrones—an *active* love.

Unfortunately, many hurting Christian parents never get down to acting out their love because they are hung up with guilt over the fact they don't always feel the love they know should be there. They go through the anguish one respected Christian author and teacher did when his unmarried daughter came home one day and said she was pregnant.

"The resentment against her was so strong my deepest feelings were closer to hatred than to love," this father confessed. "Yet I felt so wrong. I'd always preached love and had even written a book about John Wesley's concept of perfect love."

What this man came to know and what every hurting Christian parent needs to remember is that unconditional love is not always an overwhelming, uncontrollable feeling. It is more than just an emotion or a heartfelt warmth. Unconditional love is a conscious choice. And sometimes, when the feelings sag, it may be mostly resolve. It is as much a matter of the mind and will as of the heart.

Further evidence of this is the apostle Paul's description of love in 1 Corinthians 13. He didn't discuss the subject in ethereal, emotional, or philosophical terms. He defined love with a practical list of what it did or didn't do.

Henry Drummond, in *The Greatest Thing in the World,* his classic commentary on the Bible's love chapter, breaks love down into a number of ingredients. Many of these speak directly to hurting Christian parents.

Patience. Sometimes not acting is an act of love. In fact, Drummond says patience "is the normal attitude of love; love passive, love waiting to begin; not in a hurry; calm;

ready to do its work when the summons comes." That certainly describes the Farrones.

Kindness. If patience is love waiting, kindness is love active. Think about Jesus. How much of His ministry was spent doing things for the people He met? He set an example for us and then challenged us with the assurance that any kindness done "to the least of these" was the highest brand of service we could offer Him.

One mother I know, in an attempt to show her continued love for her unmarried son, sometimes takes a plate of freshly baked cookies by the apartment where he and his girlfriend live.

Kind acts take real effort and determination in the face of our hurts and concerns, but they are essential. Our expressions and claims of love ring hollow without kindness.

Humility. There is a great temptation for parents to use love to appeal to their children in order to manipulate them into conformity or guilt. The martyrdom routine does this: "Look how much I'm willing to do for you in spite of the way you've treated me."

But love that flaunts itself like that is not unconditional because it demands attention and gratitude. The love Paul writes about "does not boast." If any love is limited, it is this limelight love because its demands for notice can create resentments or barriers. Humble love is free to work gently, unoffensively behind the scenes, unencumbered by the need to be noticed.

Courtesy. Love "is not rude" is the way Paul put it. But if there is one place where a Christian's common courtesy breaks down, it is in the home. Parents often interrupt a son or daughter to get their own opinions stated. We often don't devote full attention when our children talk or extend them the courtesy of hearing them out. We are just as likely to demand and expect instant obedience. We even correct and sometimes criticize our children in front of guests in our home. In summary, we can too easily shed our manners like wet boots when we cross the threshold of our own homes.

Unselfishness. We often think of unselfishness as meaning the giving up of our rights. But unselfish, unconditional love is love without calculation.

A hurting parent can look at a son or a daughter and justifiably argue, "What about the commandment to honor parents? Doesn't he owe me some respect?" Yes, but that is the child's responsibility. If our love is truly unconditional, we will ignore those rights. We will just love unselfishly without thought about what is due us.

A most impressive example of this kind of sacrificial love is a minister and his wife who were serving a small rural church in the deep South a few years ago. They had a bright, attractive daughter who was a joy to their lives until she entered high school and began dating mostly older, more experienced boys. The more concerned her parents became about her relationships, the more rebellious and wild she became.

These parents had held high hopes for their daughter, but little by little they watched her abandon their educational dreams and goals in an attempt to melt into the provincial atmosphere of her little rural school. When she fell in love with a senior boy of questionable character and negligible ambition, her parents decided to act.

The father resigned his church and moved his family to a New England community with a highly respected school district, where his daughter could get a first-rate education and exposure to a more enriching environment. He moved despite the fact he knew he wouldn't find a church to serve. He was a self-taught man with only an eighth-grade education; and the churches in their new community required men with seminary training. So he gave up regular ministry and took other work to support his family in order to provide his daughter with the kind of environment he thought best for her.

"If we hadn't moved," said the daughter, "I'd be pumping gas and helping my husband manage some little corner station in a little Mississippi crossroads town, far from where God wants me to be."

Instead, she is a respected Christian author and speaker with a beautiful Christian family and an immense debt of gratitude to a hurting father who willingly surrendered his own career out of concern and love for her.

The kind of love that embodies all the ingredients we have mentioned—patience, kindness, humility, courtesy, and unselfishness—doesn't just happen when and if we decide we are going to be more loving. It is more a goal to aim for than it is a strategy we can easily adopt. Even with hard work and practice it is humanly impossible.

One mother voiced her frustration at the inadequacy of human love when she told me, "We have loved. We have cared until our health is broken. We have been taken advantage of. We have been robbed of possessions and money. The drug addiction gets worse than anything we ever dreamed or imagined. We're to the point now we have to guard our billfolds in our home. Sometimes the human love flees and leaves us with empty hurt. Then all we can do is cry, 'Oh, God! Give us love.'"

The Lord's brand of love is a better quality than any we could produce on our own. In 1 Corinthians 13:7 Paul claims this "love never gives up; and its faith, hope, and patience never fail" (TEV).

The best illustration I've heard in this persistent side of love involved some friends of mine—Ben and Ella Johnson. For several years after their son Jack married Sue, Ben and Ella had a warm, normal relationship with their daughter-in-law, until one day, for some inexplicable reason, Sue turned cold. She began avoiding her in-laws and refusing to communicate with them. And soon Jack, too, shut his parents out of his life.

Time after time Ben and Ella asked what was wrong,

what they had done to hurt Jack and Sue, what they could do to make it up. But there was never an explanation.

One of the hardest things for Ben and Ella to bear was the reaction of Jack and Sue's children—their own grandsons. When Ben would see the boys on the streets of their small town they would deliberately look the other way. Ella would bump into one of her grandsons in a store and he would walk away when she tried to speak to him.

For years the Christmas and birthday gifts the Johnsons sent Jack's family would be returned unopened. They tried sending cards with checks enclosed, only to have no acknowledgment and the checks not cashed.

"It was such a tightly closed door," Ben said. "But we couldn't give up."

They tried all kinds of loving gestures. Ella took them fresh bread or rolls, strawberry jam, and other things a mother enjoys sharing. But each offer was met with refusal.

"Ben and I would talk and talk, trying to imagine what we'd done," Ella said. "We were always hoping and praying our love would someday find a way to breach the empty chasm between us and our son's family. I would say, 'Ben, do you think if I would do this or ask that or take Jack and Sue some other thing, it would help?'

"Things finally came to a point where Ben responded, 'Do you just want to keep getting hurt? Don't we hurt enough?'

"But we knew we had to risk it. Neither of us wanted to give up."

After a financial crisis Jack and Sue sold their farm with plans to move hundreds of miles away. The day the moving van came, Ella went to their house once more, in a final expression of love. This time she took a box of candy for Jack's family to eat on their trip and Jack's prized old high school annuals he had left at home when he got married.

Ella's spirits soared with new hope when Jack accepted

the candy and annuals and thanked his mother. Her determined love was heartened. But when she and Ben continued to send cards and gifts for birthdays and special occasions, those expressions of love were still returned.

Three years later the Johnsons planned a long trip that was to take them through the state where Jack and Sue lived. "We couldn't think of going so near without telling them about our plans," Ella said. So she wrote a letter.

A few days later she got a reply. Sue wrote to ask them to please stop for a visit on their trip.

"What a day!" Ella said. "We cried and thanked God."

Naturally, Ben and Ella spent the first two weeks of their trip in excited anticipation of the time they would arrive at Jack and Sue's new home. Before they left their motel room on the morning of the appointed day, the Johnsons held a special time of prayer. Ben wept as he asked God to help them show their love to Jack and Sue and the grandchildren and to give them a beautiful time of reunion.

"As we drove that day, we admitted to each other our uneasiness," Ella remembered. "We wondered if Sue might wish she hadn't invited us. But we had prayed so long for that day and we knew friends were praying too. So we were confident God was preparing the way."

The minute Ben and Ella pulled into their son's driveway, their car was surrounded by the smiling faces of Jack, Sue, and the grandchildren. The entire family ushered Ben and Ella on a tour of the house and made them feel warmly welcome. The 10 years of unexplained alienation had finally ended.

Today, though the long years of hurt still remain a mystery to them, Ben and Ella have rebuilt a loving relationship with their son and his family. But neither of these long-suffering parents believes the breach could ever have been bridged without the persistent love they refused to give up.

In their struggle with despair, Ben and Ella found no human resources that could supply the kind of unconditional love they needed to get through to their son and daughter-in-law. But they found, as any hurting Christian parent who asks can find, that God has an abundant supply of love. And He is willing to supply all we can use.

Paul wrote about this love source when he said:

> I pray that Christ will be more and more at home in your hearts, living within you as you trust in Him. May your roots go down deep into the soil of God's marvelous love; and may you be able to feel and understand, as all God's children should, how long, how wide, how deep, and how high his love really is; and to experience this love for yourselves, though it is so great that you will never see the end of it or fully know or understand it. And so at last you will be filled up with God himself *(Ephesians 3:17-19, TLB)*.

That is the only secret to the kind of unconditional love that can have an impact on the lives of our children.

Chapter 9

Helping the Outcast Parent

by Dan Collins

Background Scripture: Luke 10:25-37; Galatians 6:2

YOUR DAUGHTER, DANIELLE,* is in one of my classes this year," a college professor said to me one Sunday morning.

"That's what she tells me," I replied.

"Yes," the teacher continued, "she's a fine student. Speaks right up in class."

"That's Danielle. We must be talking about the same person. She's never at a loss for words."

No surprises so far in the conversation with Dr. Smith following the worship service. But one was not far away, hidden like a land mine.

"Danielle had some very complimentary things to say about you the other day in class."

"Oh?" was all I could say—half surprised, half embarrassed. In the awkward silence that followed Dr. Smith added,

"She is a tribute to your parenting skills. You've done an excellent job as a parent. You have earned the right to be proud."

Before I could answer he was called away. I was left alone with my thoughts.

I smiled.

Then just as quickly as it came the smile faded and was replaced by a tear. As casually as I could I brushed it away with the back of my hand. I hoped no one noticed. I didn't want to explain either the smile or the tear. Both had come as this thought raced through my mind:

If you had been around here a few years ago, Dr. Smith, you never would have talked about my parenting skills. Most people who were in the church back then were sure I didn't have any. For you see, Dr. Smith, in those days we were having a lot of trouble with Danielle's older brother, Danny.

I turned away, physically. As if I could put that chapter behind me forever. But it didn't work. Just the thought of those tragic experiences caused all the old emotions to surface once again.

Daniel Alexander Collins III.

Too much name for a little boy. But we were so excited when Danny was born, and my father was so proud when we passed on his name to his first grandson. We had no illusions about parenting. We knew we were rookies. But we were confident we would succeed where others had failed. We weren't perfect. Our son would have his faults. But he would grow up to love the Lord and be a credit to his family. His grandfather would always have reason to be proud of his grandson.

But somewhere along the way the dream faded. Teenage rebellion destroyed peace in our home and dashed our hopes for the future. Bitter words, drugs, crime, jail became the realities of life. Our son had become a stranger.

We had no idea where he went each evening. Sometimes he wouldn't return until the next day. We longed for sleep that would not come; daily we prayed for the strength to survive the waking hours. We ceased to be productive people, looking only for ways to reduce the pain that engulfed us, pain that would not go away and from which we could not hide.

Excommunicated by Silence

I should have been prepared for what happened next. After all, I've been around the church all my life. Most of my adult years have been spent in some leadership role in the church. I know the church. I know how it acts and reacts.

I should have been prepared for what happened as soon as Danny's reputation became known in the church. But I wasn't.

Danny was excluded by the "best" families in the church. Parents told their daughters, "You are never to ride with Danny again. If you don't have a ride home from the party, call me. But never get in the same car with Danny."

That was probably unnecessary advice. Danny was no longer being invited to private parties and had largely quit attending church functions. There appeared to be a conscious conspiracy: Ignore him and he will go away.

So they did, and he did.

Danny got phone calls, but not from anyone associated with the church. No one. Not the senior pastor. Not the youth pastor. Not even his Sunday School teacher. The people who called wouldn't give their names if he wasn't home. And soon he wasn't home a lot. As far as the church was concerned, Danny ceased to exist.

But that didn't surprise me. After all, Danny had become the kind of person I wouldn't let him associate with.

I was shocked into numbness by the realization that my wife and I were being punished for the actions of our son. Since he did not live up to the expectations of the religious community, we were emotionally excommunicated. Clearly we were being held responsible for his anti-social actions.

The rejection was quite subtle. The punishment could be summed up in one word.

Silence.

No longer were we asked to go out for coffee after the evening service. No one called to find out why we were not present for Sunday School. When sleep didn't come until after 4 A.M. on a Sunday morning it was nearly impossible to follow a regular schedule. But no one seemed to care. At least that's how it seemed when the phone did not ring.

Nor did anyone talk with us at church very much. For a while we stood around the foyer after service until nearly everyone had left. But few stopped to talk. And those who did talked only about the weather or the football scores. Danny's name was not mentioned. He was an outcast, he did not exist anymore. Before long we started leaving church immediately following the service.

My work takes me out of town often. Before one trip I could not cancel, I asked several people to call my wife while I was gone. I knew it would be a tough week for her. Thursday morning I phoned her. Things were worse than I feared. I cancelled everything and flew home. Later I learned that no one, not one person, called my wife while I was away.

Punishment by isolation. At least that is how it seemed to us.

During those desperate months I was involved in speaking engagements that took me from the Atlantic to the Pacific coasts. Every time I dropped a hint about Danny I would have many people talk to me after the service. They, too, were having trouble with a child. They, too, were being punished. The leadership of the church said to hurting parents things like:

"I'm sure you won't mind being replaced; I know you have a lot of things on your mind at this time."

Or, "This job needs to be done by a parent who has a child in the teen group."

Others discovered they were not reappointed to the Sunday School class they had taught for several years, or their name did not appear on the ballot at the annual meetings. These parents were being held responsible for the sinful choices of their children.

The Loneliest Time of My Life

The period of isolation was the loneliest time in my life. During those months I heard a parent say, "I didn't know you could hurt as much as you hurt for a child." To which I wanted to add, "especially if you are hurting alone."

Soon I discovered, however, that loneliness with all its devastation is less painful than rejection.

Both my wife and I were reared in homes where church attendance was the highest priority on the calendar. All our married life we had followed the same pattern. Soon, however, we became irregular in our attendance. On reflection I must admit—not all the distance that developed between us and the church can be charged to others. We took a big step back from the Christian fellowship. We, too, must accept some of the blame.

We were embarrassed. After all, we were failures. Danny was a loser, well on his way to a tragic collision with the law. It hurt to talk about him. Tears swelled up in the eyes. A lump grew in the throat. It was toughest around "successful" parents.

And guilty. Often we asked ourselves, Where did we go

wrong? We analyzed and dissected the decisions we had made throughout Danny's life. What should we have done differently? We wanted to know. We needed to know so we would not repeat the mistakes with Danielle. But we couldn't face reality. We didn't want to talk about it.

We were numb. The nights were too dark, too long. There was never enough sleep. We were tired, confused, angry, troubled—and scared. Every siren sent chills up the spine; panic every time a police car drove by the house. We were afraid to read newspaper stories of drug-related arrests, and yet were drawn irresistibly to them.

Most of all there was grief. Like death, only worse. The teenage son of a friend of mine died of leukemia. I knew that had to be tough. Yet I remember crying out to God in the darkness through my tears, "Why couldn't Danny have died from leukemia? At least it would be over. At least someone would care. At least I could talk about it. I wouldn't have to hide. That would be a respectable way to lose a son."

Several years have now passed since those days of intense pain. Some bad things, and some very good things have taken place. I wish I could tell you about them. But out of courtesy to Danny I'd better not. You'll be pleased to know, I'm sure, that Danny is putting his life back together again.

No one can experience what we did and be the same. Out of the distillation of those months come these observations. They are shared humbly with the church and with parents in pain.

A Place to Begin

What can the church do?

A church can and should do all the distinctly religious things. Like prayer. Lots of prayer.

But this is not enough.

Hurting parents need positive expressions of caring. Some people in the church may have to be tough enough to take some psychic blows from injured parents and keep coming back. Very likely love will be tested to see if it is real. It is, unfortunately, easier to ignore the problem of the hurting parents than it is to invest the time, energy, and emotion to listen to their story and to share their heartbreak.

If you choose to help, be nonjudgmental, both with the child and the parent. Recognize that these are difficult days for young people. Be humble enough to admit you don't know the whole story. A pair of 15-year-olds I know of were found having intercourse behind the piano in a Sunday School room in a holiness church. Indignant parents succeeded in having the boy banned from the teen group. The teens knew, however, that while the boy was a willing partner, it was the "nice" girl who was sexually aggressive.

Be quietly grateful if your children have "turned out all right." Remember, there but for the grace of God . . .

Most of all, parents in pain need someone who is willing to stand by, be available, listen when they need to talk, and cry with them when no words will come.

What should the hurting parent do?

Keep in mind that these words are shared by a fellow-traveler who wishes now he had done these things.

Seek out someone with whom you can talk, a prayer partner, a support in tough times. Be honest enough to admit that some of the isolation came because you stepped back from the Christian fellowship.

Stay close to the church. Attend regularly. Keep your devotional life active. Maintain open dialogue with your spouse. Let the people know, by your actions, that you are willing to talk about your wayward child. What may seem like emotional excommunication may in fact be a reluctance to bring any more pain to you.

Keep the lines of communication open with your "Danny." Be understanding, supportive, and caring. Be tough if necessary. Sometimes children learn how to stand only if you allow them to fall. Let it be known that your love is never in question. Let them know that, while they can break your heart, they can never destroy your love for them.

Keep the family going. Other children must not suffer from the family sorrow any more than is absolutely necessary.

Join a support group if one is available in your neighborhood.

Most of all be aware that the important question is not, Why? but, Where do I go from here? God's love and grace can work miracles when hope is gone and dreams are smashed. Danny's story is a testimony that there are no final failures with God.

But we'll have to talk about that another time.

*Names in this story have been changed, as has the name of the author. The events took place as described. The author is an ordained elder in a holiness church.

Chapter 10

When Teens Start Doing More than Just Thinking About Sex

by Gary Sivewright

Background Scripture: 1 Thessalonians 4:1-8

IT'S A FACT. Teenagers are becoming more promiscuous.

But not *our* teenagers—not those in the church? Guess again.

For years we have known that teens have been getting more and more sexually active. But we churchgoers have reacted smugly. We thought most of this sexual activity was taking place among teens outside the church.

We have a few bad apples among our youth, we thought, but for the most part, they're clean, innocent kids. Well, they might be clean, but they are no longer innocent.

In a recent survey among 2,000 teens in evangelical churches, we discovered some alarming news.[1] Nearly 1 in 4 have already had sexual intercourse. And 1 in 3 have been involved in fondling of genitals.

Statistics are often boring. But I think you'll find these startling.[2] Here are a few of the questions we asked the teens, along with a tally of their responses.

Which of the following have you done with a member of the opposite sex:

	Yes	No
Hold hands	90%	8%
Embracing and some kissing	80%	18%
Heavy "french" kissing	62%	35%
Fondling of breasts	42%	54%
Fondling of genitals	33%	62%
Sexual intercourse	23%	74%

For two people who are not married but are both willing, the following actions are morally acceptable:

	Yes	No
Hold hands	98%	1%
Embracing and some kissing	96%	3%
Heavy "french" kissing	82%	10%
Fondling of breasts	41%	42%
Fondling of genitals	34%	49%
Sexual intercourse	25%	64%

How much of your information about sex and sexual relations have you received from:

	A lot	Some	A little	None
Parents	23%	35%	27%	14%
Brothers/sisters	9%	19%	18%	53%
Friends	37%	34%	21%	8%
Books	17%	32%	28%	23%
Classes at school	23%	31%	25%	21%
Church	6%	20%	31%	43%
Movies	26%	33%	27%	14%
Television	21%	32%	32%	15%
"Adult" sex- oriented magazines	11%	10%	20%	59%
The Bible	11%	23%	29%	36%

Television and movies have as much influence in shaping the sexual values of teens as do parents. But none of these have as much influence as friends. And where are these friends getting their values? Television and movies, to a great extent.

A year-after-year barrage of visual images that spotlight distorted values can erode our beliefs. They can convince us that unwholesome behavior depicted on the screen is not so unwholesome after all.

In the area of sexual relationships, those influences can make it difficult to determine the difference between love and lust. Of course, love is giving up our selfish desires to make life better for someone else. Lust is the fulfillment of our desire to exclusion or hurt of someone else.

Teens learn the real meaning of love from role models— like actors, musicians, or their own parents. Because of this, we parents must demonstrate our love for our spouse. Teens need to see, inside their own homes, that love and sex within marriage is not a dirty word, but can be and should be enjoyed.

Quest for Sexual Identity

Parents should not only show their teens what it is like to be part of a marriage based on love. Parents should demonstrate their acceptance of the teen during those years when the teen begins the quest for sexual identity—that is, their search to discover how to translate sex into their daily lives.

We demonstrate this acceptance by loving them and liking them. (You have to love them to get to heaven. You must like them to live peacefully with them).

It can be difficult to do either one until we realize that teenagers go through stages where they press all limits, including the sexual. Their search for sexual identity will show up in dating (or dreaming of dating), clothes, make-up, hairstyles, reading material, viewing material, music, and sexual fantasy.

Instead of taking up a hands-on-the-hips judgmental attitude, parents should force themselves to remember that they, too, had to come to grips with their own sexuality. I use the word "force" because many of us have unpleasant memories we would just as soon leave dead and buried. But if we can resurrect some of those experiences, along with the emotion, pain, and confusion buried with them, it becomes easier to understand what our teens are going through.

Sex is scary, frustrating, defeating, and perplexing. It is also fun and exciting. We parents must accept the fact that our teenagers are growing up in a world that reeks with sexploitation. Shapely women and sun-bronzed hunks pander everything from condoms to hair spray to dog food.

Because of our sex-oriented age, which has warped many of the traditional values we taught our children, teens are called upon to make some difficult decisions. When I was a teenager, we had to decide whether or not to kiss on the first date. Many teens today have to decide whether or not they'll have sex on the first date.

I know of a young man who picked up his date, a young lady he had never gone out with before. As they walked to the car she said, "You might as well know right now that if you aren't planning on this date ending in bed, then I'm going to turn around and go right back into my house."

He wasn't, so she did.

Our teens do have some tough decisions to make. And they will not always make the decisions we would want them to make. But as parents we must appreciate the fact that our sons and daughters are maturing. And we must show them that we *like them anyway*.

Taking Time to Listen

Another thing. Teens need parents to take the time to listen and to show concern.

Recently one teen in a small discussion group I sat in on said, "I wish my father would just once take the time to tell me he appreciates me." Our survey told us that parents are taking very little time to talk with their teens about things that matter most.

On the average, fathers spend less than 15 minutes a week in meaningful conversation with their children; mothers less than 30 minutes. Yet teens need time, and not just time spent in the same house under the same roof. Time to talk about what is important to them.

In one of the most tragic cases of communication problems I've ever witnessed, it wasn't what the parents said that caused the problem. It was what they didn't say or do. I was the minister to two teen sisters who had nothing good to say about their parents. As I got to know the girls better, I realized the problem wasn't all their fault.

They were disruptive, obnoxious, and occasionally destructive. But they came to every church activity. When we organized a basketball team, they were the first to join. What surprised me was that the parents, good Christian people, never attended a single game. Not once did they come to watch their girls play. I found out later that they never went to a high school concert either, though both girls sang in the choir.

When the parents chose not to get involved in the lives of their daughters, the girls interpreted that to mean they didn't care. And it's kind of hard to talk about important issues, such as sex, with people who don't seem to care about you.

Parents at the End of Their Rope

Parents must understand their role as belayers. That's a mountain climber's term identifying those who secure a person who is hanging at the end of a rope.

My first (and last) time mountain climbing, I discovered how important the belayer is. As I hung halfway down a mountainside, dangling at the end of a reinforced kite string, the belayer would shout instructions and encouragement to me. He did not govern my speed, but he could stop my fall if I lost control. A belayer doesn't have to be an expert, but from his perspective he can see things the climber cannot.

A girl came up to me after one of my camp talks on parent-teen relationships. "I want you to know how wonderful my parents are," she said. "It seems like after 18 years I'm just now able to see how much they've had to put up with." "What's more," she confessed, "I'm understanding that they're not perfect, but they've tried to be the best parents they could. We're friends now."

I thought, There are some parents who have learned the fine art of belaying, and a teen who just now understands she has been belayed.

There are at least two things a belayer should not do:

1. The belayer should not do the work for the climber by just pulling the climber up.

2. The belayer should not cut the rope (no matter how tempting it might be).

Dan Croy, in the book *Parents, Teens, and Other Strangers* (Beacon Hill), writes "Remember, whether you are a climber or belayer, no one said this would be easy. Becoming an adult is often a frustrating and painful experience." Loving children and then giving them the slack they need to climb on their own can be a terrifying and painful scene for a parent to watch. Specific directions from the belayer to the climber on where to step next or how to maneuver the ledge can spark some intense exchanges of words. But survival of the climber depends not on following his own instincts or even in following every piece of advice from the belayer. Survival depends on teamwork.

This teamwork reveals itself in a willingness to discuss problems—to talk openly and to learn from one another. One of the problems many parents are not comfortable talking to their teens about is sex. Part of the difficulty may be that many of us parents are not comfortable with our own sexuality.

What we need to convey to our teens is that sex is a marvelous, wonderful, enjoyable, and sometimes mysterious gift from God. It is not to be perverted by the using and abusing of people which devalues their humanity. In addition, we need to help our teens realize that sex is best when it is enjoyed within the context of the marriage bond. Anything less is a cheap substitute for the real thing.

Because many parents are a bit intimidated by the thought of talking with their teens about sex, it can be helpful to have discussion starters. Something to encourage parents and teens to talk together.

By discussion starter, I don't mean the *Playboy* magazine you found hidden under your son's mattress while hosing down his room. Nor do I mean the news from your neighbor that your daughter has seen the last three R-rated features at the local cinema.

This is not to say that positive discussions cannot come out of some of these negative confrontations. To turn the negatives into a positives, just replace judgmental questions like "What do you think Jesus thinks about all this?" and "Do you know how this makes your mother and me feel?" to "What are you learning from all this?" or "How are women and men portrayed?"

A few positive discussion starters I would suggest are the Josh McDowell "Why Wait" video, or any of the following books: *Next Time I Fall in Love* by Chap Clark (Youth Specialties); *Worth the Wait* by Tim Stafford (Campus Life); and *Sex . . . Desiring the Best* by St. Clair and Jones (Here's Life).

If parents and teens can agree to talk together about things that matter, even if they have to schedule the time on their calendars, they'll be miles ahead in their relationship. Using these resources as springboards, parents can talk with their sons and daughters about the joys of sex as well as the dangers it poses.

Talking with Your Teen About Sex

Josh McDowell, in his book *How to Help Your Child Say No to Sexual Pressure* (Word), identifies a host of reasons to say no to premarital sex. And he categorizes the reasons into four major areas: physical, spiritual, emotional, and relational.

Physically, teens face not only the dangers of pregnancy and sexually transmitted disease. There's also the danger of addiction. Because sex is so enjoyable, it's a bit like a narcotic.

Spiritually, illicit sex breaks our fellowship with God. "It is God's will that you should be sanctified: that you should avoid sexual immorality; that each of you should learn to control his own body" (1 Thessalonians 4:3-4). Teens who engage in sex often suffer not only the loss of God's fellowship but also they can lose respect for themselves (because they failed to control their body) and for their partner.

Emotionally, there is the problem of guilt that comes from realizing we violated God's standards. In addition, teens can suffer from reruns of mental videotapes from past sexual encounters with other partners. And this can leave them feeling dirty when they are with their new friend.

Relationally, because sex is addictive, there's a real danger that much of the teen couple's private time will be spent in physical exploration. This is the very time they should be talking about their goals in life and their feelings about events and people around them. But sex can cut short the communication upon which well-rounded relationships must be built.

Arm Your Teen

McDowell, in the same book, offers some replies your teen can use when he or she is being pressured to have sex. Here are a few.

If you love me, you'll have sex with me.

Reply: If you love me, you'll respect my feelings and not push me into doing something I'm not ready for.

If you don't, someone else will.

Reply: If all I mean to you is a body to have sex with, maybe we'd better take a closer look at why we see each other. You have no right to use me.

Don't you want to try it to see what it's like:

Reply: What is this? Some kind of commercial ad? Try it; you'll like it! I do plan to try it with my husband (wife).

Sex will cause our love to grow.

Reply: But into what?

To love you so much and hold back hurts!

Reply: Love is worth some sacrifice.

Spiritually, teens cannot serve two masters. If they allow their sex drive to control their emotions and actions, there is not much room for Christ's control. Sexual fantasies are common among even Christian teenage men and women. But when those fantasies begin to monopolize their thoughts and influence their behavior, trouble lies not far ahead.

God is not the eternal party pooper. He is the Author and Creator of life, and He knows best how it is to be lived and enjoyed. If we can help our teens understan⁁ this about God, and if we can help them see sex as part of the healthy relationship between husband and wife, we will have scaled a huge stumbling block to the spiritual maturity we want so much for our teens.

---

1. *The Josh McDowell Ministry "Why Wait?" Study on Teen Sexuality in the Evangelical Church* was conducted among about 2,000 teens in American, evangelical churches. Among participating churches were holiness denominations such as the Church of the Nazarene, The Wesleyan Church, and the Free Methodist Church. The study was directed by Barna Research Group of Glendale, Calif., during the summer of 1987.

2. As you review these numbers, you might keep in mind that responses from the general population, in similar surveys, on the average, run only about 10 percent higher on the side of promiscuity than do these responses. For example, while 23 percent of evangelical teens say they have had intercourse, about 33 percent of teens in general have had intercourse.

Gary Sivewright is director of Nazarene Youth International for the Church of the Nazarene. He is a husband and a father. His sons are 10 and 7.

Chapter 11

Suicide:
The Most Tragic Death of All

by Frances Simpson

Background Scripture: Matthew 27:1-5; John 10:10;
Philippians 4:10-14

MAHATMA GANDHI, honored by the people of India as the father of their nation, decided to kill himself when he was 14.

He and a friend had reached the conclusion they could no longer endure the oppressive British rule and the lack of independence. So, in sheer disgust, they decided to commit suicide. They hiked into the jungle in search of poisonous seeds from a rare bush. But when they found them, their courage began to fail.

Suppose we do not die quickly? they thought. What would it accomplish anyway?

Both went ahead and swallowed a few seeds, then fought off the sickness to stay alive. Later they composed themselves and discarded their plan to kill themselves.

Suicide is a nightmare that has spanned the centuries. It just won't go away. And it affects people of all ages, not only older folks who seek an escape from the pains of age. In the United States alone, over 1,000 young people try to kill themselves every day. About 7,000 will succeed this year. The suicide rate among 15- to 24-year-olds has nearly tripled in the last 25 years.

What Are the Signs?

It is difficult to know, in advance, who will attempt suicide. Though people who are suicidal share many characteristics, some suicides can be attributed to the immaturity of youth or to the senility of the aged. But for the moment let's talk about suicidal people who don't appear to be immature or senile.

People who consider suicide commonly experience an overwhelming sense of hopelessness. Often they feel a terrible loneliness that isolates them from everything and everyone. Life seems to lose its value. Death becomes an escape, a refuge from pain.

Many of those contemplating suicide paint verbal warning signs.

"What would you say if I took my own life?"

"Well, I won't always be around to bother you." Other warning signs are:

- Severe mood changes
- A sudden decline in performance, whether at school or work

- Excessive, unexplainable fatigue
- Sudden improvement in behavior, suggesting relief that the troubles will soon be over
- Loss of interest in hobbies and other activities that once seemed important
- Neglect of personal appearance
- Making final arrangements, such as giving away treasures and making lists of who gets what
- A reluctance to talk about the future
- Hearing unearthly voices and experiencing other abnormal phenomena
- The inability to think clearly and make decisions

Why Do Some People Kill Themselves?

There are, on occasion, impulsive suicides prompted by a kind of temporary insanity, an intense desire that overrides the person's usual character and emotional state.

Most suicides, however, have been linked to deep depression.

Winston Churchill, a long-time sufferer of depression, called it "the Black Dog." If this Black Dog remains with us for two weeks or more, we can be pretty certain what we're seeing is something other than the Monday morning blues most of us experience.

What causes this industrial-strength depression?

Genetics, for one. Science has revealed that a disruption in the delicate interplay of chemicals in the brain can cause what is clinically defined as major depression. In addition, drugs and alcohol can further disrupt the chemical balance and heighten the depression.

What are some other causes of depression?

Tendency toward depression increases with age, especially among those who have weak relationships with others.

The highly competitive society in which we live creates stress, which, in turn, can cause depression.

Studies show that those without religious values appear to be more prone to suicide. For example, according to studies by Professor Steven Stack at Pennsylvania State University, the rate of teenage suicide is much lower among teens who attend church than among those who don't.

Traumatic events such as broken romances, family arguments, divorce, problems at work or school, or illness can trigger a suicide attempt.

Another cause of depression and suicide stems from our secular society, which revolves around Hollywood, rock stars, and self. This exclusion of God breeds hopelessness and despair.

I know of a Christian teenager I'll call Ellen. She was a brilliant young lady. Yet she slit her wrist 50 times at a teen retreat.

Her counselor later said, "Ninety percent of the cause can be attributed to the music she listened to." For hours at a time, Ellen would sit in her closet with earphones on, listening to her collection of more than 400 hard rock records. Lyrics like, "When you're bad, you're bad," and "Cut yourself and bleed," slowly nudged her mind into a black tunnel.

Almost all suicidal people have trouble with personal relationships. So when they find someone with whom they feel comfortable, then lose that person, despair can take control.

Consider the case of Michelle, for example. She was a missionary's child. And like most missionary kids, she moved a lot. Because friends came and went, her constant inner cry was, "Don't leave. Please, someone love me."

Michelle's parents were loving and caring. How could she explain that their love wasn't enough, that she desperately needed another kind of love? In the 10th grade Michelle met David, a senior, and life took on new meaning. But when David left for college in the States, Michelle's world fell apart. At first she battled violently, trying to prove she could survive without him. But before long the depression overtook her.

Michelle walked down to the pond where David had first held her hand. She sat on the soft grass, hoping the tears and sobs would drive away the pain. But it didn't. Unable to resist the suicidal thoughts that engulfed her, she waded into the pond. It wasn't until she stood waist-deep in the icy water that she came to her senses.*

What Can We Do?

If you are worried that someone you know is thinking about suicide, talk with that person about your concerns. People thinking about suicide are usually relieved that someone notices something is wrong and wants to help. The best thing to do is communicate.

Avoid making moral judgments. Realize that these people really hurt. Let them know that you recognize this. Assure them that the painful feeling will go away.

If someone has threatened suicide, contact them daily. Involve other people. Surround them with their peers. Suicidal people need friends to support them in overcoming problems and getting through emotional bad times.

People suffering from major depression have more trouble overcoming problems than do most people. Because of this, we should be as concerned about helping our troubled friends learn nondestructive approaches to their difficulties as we are in preventing them from killing themselves.

Sometimes, in spite of all that family and friends can do, emotional stress seems to take control of the person. In such situations, therapy or medical treatment is necessary. If the problem is caused by chemical imbalances, it can usually be treated with great success.

Some mental health experts feel that research will eventually show that most depression has genetic or internal chemical causes. Others believe that depression has its roots in the human spirit. Most experts, however, both secular and Christian, believe depression can be caused by one, or the other, or a combination of the two.

Various support groups across the country are doing more than wringing their hands and asking, "What went wrong?" They are asking, "What can we do?"

Suicide crisis centers are springing up around the country. Films, such as *The Question,* by Mars Hills Productions in Houston, are being used to educate the masses. Billboards, such as the one I saw in Clear Lake, Iowa, scream, "Suicide is NOT the answer. Call 537-HELP."

What About Those Left Behind?

"All right," you say, "that's well and good. But someone I love has already committed suicide. Where do I go from here?"

Suicide causes a degree of shock and grief among the survivors that can't be matched by any other form of bereavement. When a loved one dies of a fatal illness, we exhaust all medical sources, then say, "We did all we could." If they die in an accident, we can usually admit, "There was nothing I could do."

But with suicide, the "whys" haunt us. Why my daughter? My son? My wife? My dad? My friend? Could I have contributed to it? Could I have prevented it? We don't like the silence that follows these questions. Tidal waves of guilt sweep over family and friends.

We need to remember that this is part of the grief process. You probably did all you could.

Remember, too, that God is in control. All the "whys" we cannot answer, we can trust to the goodness and mercy and justice of God.

Ben Huston, pastor, youth worker, counselor, and father of four, sighed to his wife one evening. "I've given all I can. I don't have any more to give." A few days later he hanged himself with an extension cord from the winding staircase of the church parsonage.

The family couldn't believe it. "That wasn't Ben. Ben wouldn't do that. He's talked others out of doing that very thing."

On the Sunday afternoon of the funeral, a soloist sang Ben's favorite song, "If I Had a Thousand Lives to Live, I'd Live Them All for Jesus."

"Whys" hung like shrouds in the hearts of Ben's wife and teenage children. "Whys" lurked in the minds of the 200 ministers scattered throughout the auditorium. And "whys" echoed across the town and around the state.

Mid sobs throughout the building, the district superintendent began to read his text for the funeral message, "and the vessel that he made of clay was marred in the hand of the potter" (Jeremiah 18:4, KJV). The congregation understood. Ben was not perfect. He was fallible. And for a moment, at least, more fallible than most.

Sometime later I asked his wife, Ruth, "What helped you through that difficult time?"

"The Lord did it," she answered. "If it hadn't been for the Lord, I couldn't have gone through it. The church people helped too . . . and my family."

Perhaps the best way to comfort those who have lost a loved one by suicide is in the same way we comfort anyone who loses someone.

- Pray for the family
- Send flowers or donate to a favorite charity
- Look for an immediate need and fill it
- Be there when needed
- Don't offer advice unless it is asked for
- Let loved ones express their grief
- Don't be afraid to touch

Take heart. For those suffering from deep depression, and for those who are left grieving in the wake of the suicide of a loved one, Jesus has said, "I have come that they may have life, and have it to the full" (John 10:10). That's a promise worth taking seriously.

---

*Michelle Phoenix, "What Is Wrong with Me?" *U* (March 1988): 3-5.

Frances Simpson is a free-lance writer, and the wife of a district superintendent in the Church of the Nazarene, Charlotte, N.C.

Chapter 12

Stepfamilies, Keeping in Step

by Jack M. Barnell

Background Scripture: Proverbs 22:6; Romans 13:8-10;
Ephesians 6:4

EXCITEMENT RAN HIGH on that front pew as our children squirmed. They were ages 1, 3, and 5. And they were watching us marry.

For my wife and me it was a new beginning. We had both lost our first spouses in death.

We expected to blend my son with her son and daughter into a first-marriage kind of a family. Now that our children are grown, we know just how unrealistic that expectation was.

Stepfamilies are beset with problems typical families never have to face. Given those problems, and given the fact that over 35 million Americans live in stepfamilies, let's think about this question: How can Christians in stepfamilies deal effectively with the unique problems they face, and at the same time keep in step with God's Spirit?

The Mark of Cain—Stepfamily Stigma

When you belong to a stepfamily, you wear something not a great deal unlike the mark of Cain. It sets you apart from the rest of the world and makes others suspicious of you. Why?

It has to do with the fact that stepfamilies are born out of loss. At least one spouse or parent has been lost through death or divorce. Out of this loss comes one of what can be many forms of stepfamilies, also called blended, remarried, reconstituted, or aggregate families. But no matter what form the stepfamily takes, it will usually include at least one previously married spouse and a child. An exception would be when a child is born out of wedlock.

Stepfamilies have more players than first-marriage families. These players—such as children of a divorced couple—move in and out of the family's scene. They are blood-related to only some members, may have different last names, may call parenting adults by names other than Mom and Dad, and always seem to have a complicated extended family.

All of these variations tend to label stepfamilies as "different." And society usually treats differentness with suspicion.

When the Roll Is Called—Who's There?

Most children call their parents "Mom" and "Dad" or some variation of these names. But when couples remarry, names get complicated. Children ask, "Should I call Dad's new wife 'Mom' or 'Hazel'?" Some stepparents measure their acceptance by whether or not stepchildren call them "Mom" or "Dad." In most cases, this is an unfair measure.

Wise stepparents approach names cautiously. Relationships are more important than names. A stepparent's victory on the name is rather hollow if he receives only contempt from the child.

Stepparents should also approach last names with care. When my wife's son started school, he had a different last name than my son. But we didn't want him to face complications over that, such as the presumption that his mom and dad were divorced. So I adopted my wife's son and daughter.

Stepparents should weigh the pros and cons of name changes. Will adoption be best, or hyphenated names of birth and present parent, or no change at all?

Land of the Free—Territorial Rights

"I don't want to share my room with a kid I don't know!" Jason shouted at his mom. "This is my room. Eric can sleep in the basement!"

Jason was the son of a lady I know who was planning on marrying the father of eight-year-old Eric. The stepfather and his boy were then going to move into the two-bedroom house of Jason and his mom. But Jason did not want to give up the privacy of his own bedroom. He didn't want Eric to invade his space.

Stepfamilies have a space problem. If they move into a house already occupied by some of their members, then they can expect at least some resentment and tension. "This is my room" or "What are you doing in my chair?" may not be said, but it is often felt.

Another reason stepfamilies clash is because of the remaining possessions of the departed spouse. One remarried wife complained to me, "Every time I turn around, I'm reminded of Dale's first wife. We have her furniture sitting just like it was when she was here. We eat from her dishes, sleep in her bed, and even have her picture on the wall. When I say to Dale, 'Let's buy something new,' he just looks hurt then says, 'We can't afford it now.' What he really means is, 'I can't bear to lose her memory.' But I feel like I don't even count."

How can Christian stepfamilies deal with territorial rights? A good starting point is Christ's basic principle for all relationships: "Love your neighbor as yourself." In addition, when the marriage has been planned, spouses-to-be should call a family council meeting. This should include all children affected by the marriage.

Topics to be discussed should include where the family will live, joint possessions, and who gets which rooms. Money certainly sets limits on options. If possible, the family should choose living arrangements that are new to everyone. But if both spouses are from the same school district, it will help if the move stays within that district, to preserve friendships for the children.

If it is not possible to move into a residence new to everyone, then the family must decide how to share living quarters already occupied by some family members. Parents can lead the meeting, but ideas and opinions of all should be respected. After careful discussion, family members will try to agree on the best solutions. A parent should open and close the meeting with prayer.

Perhaps you are right now in a stepfamily where territorial rights are causing chaos. You can still call a family council meeting, air the problems, and seek God's guidance for solutions.

One final word on territory relates to stepchildren who only occasionally live with non-custodial parents. It is better to say, "Lonnie is living here today" (or this weekend) than to say, "Lonnie is visiting today." Saying the child *lives* here, even for a day or a month, tends to suggest greater stability and makes the child feel more welcome.

The child also needs a place to keep personal things. It may be a drawer, a chest, or a room. These personal things should stay in this house so the child always has some familiar things when he comes to live. By having a place and possessions at each household, the child may feel more secure.

Who's in Charge?—Discipline

"Don't tell me what to do," shouted 15-year-old Kent at his stepmom. "You're not my mother!" He slammed the door and charged out of the house. Marie watched his retreating form through the window. You're right, she thought. I'm not your Mom. But you live here some of the time and I insist on obedience.

Marie and Dan had married two years before. Kent had lived with his mom, but then he started skipping school. He began smoking pot and drinking beer with his friends. Finally his mom sent him to live with Marie and Dan. They already had Marie's 14-year-old son and 10-year-old daughter from her previous marriage. Then there was a 3-year-old girl who was born to Marie and Dan.

Marie was concerned about Kent's influence on her children, especially her son. She expected Dan to set limits for Kent. But Dan seemed unsure of himself. He was too eager to accept Kent's explanation for breaking the rules. Dan needed Kent's love and approval and thought he could get it by overlooking his misbehavior.

So Marie charged in to handle the discipline problem. And that ended with Kent storming out of the house.

Most children learn how to get their way with parents. But children in stepfamilies can be even more skilled in this. They often deal with a parent who feels guilty over the breakup of the first marriage. This parent wants approval from the child, to affirm that the child doesn't blame the parent for the broken marriage. This parent may end up "buying" approval from the child by giving in on discipline issues.

Parents must protect a child from harm and prepare the child for adulthood. In first-marriage families, parents don't always agree on how to do this. In stepfamilies, disagreements are often sharper. The birth parent may overlook obnoxious behavior in a child "because of all he's been through." The non-birth parent sees the behavior as attention-getting, as an effort to grab power, or as an attempt to break up the new marriage.

Stepparents need to discuss differences in parenting style. As far as possible, each birth parent should discipline his child. Later, as the marriage grows more secure and children accept stepparents, authority may be shared. Discipline still must be done in love, not in anger. And it should be based on mutual respect.

The family council meeting can be used to help stepparents in the art of discipline. Major family rules may be hammered out in the council. Keep rules few. Make sure they are understood. Set consequences for breaking rules. Consequences should be reasonable and enforceable. See that they affect the rule-breaker most, rather than inconveniencing the whole family.

When a rule is broken, parents must enforce the consequence. In this way they say, "You broke the rule. Therefore, you chose the consequence. We respect your right to make that choice." By allowing the consequence, the child's right to choose is accepted. The stepparent is not the culprit.

Tug-of-war—Loyalty Issues

Barbara was upset. Her 13-year-old son and 10-year-old daughter had just returned from a weekend with Barbara's ex-husband and his new wife. The boy said, "Wow! You should see their new house—pool, tennis court, and Jacuzzi." The girl piped up, "Sue let me help her make cookies. And we sewed some clothes for my doll. It was fun!"

Barbara really shouldn't have gotten upset—a tad bit jealous maybe, but not upset. Different households have different facilities and different ways of doing things. And different doesn't necessarily mean better or worse.

When children return from living with parents who don't have custody of them, the step- and custodial parents can find it helpful to ask their children what they liked best about their stay. In this way the parents can find out what things were done differently in the other household. By asking about the children's experiences, parents may defuse some of the emotion connected with the differences. It is not helpful to pry information out of children, however. Rather, allow them to share only what they want to tell.

Stepparents and birth parents should say kind things about absent parents. You may disagree with things they do, but don't belittle them. They are important to your children, and to Christ. When you speak well of these absent parents, you express God's love. It also decreases for the children tensions about which parent to be loyal to. The children can have good times with all parents without betraying the love they have for any of those parents.

Successful stepfamilies allow looser boundaries in relationships than do nuclear families. There has to be room for more people in stepfamilies. There may be more than one mom or dad, more brothers and sisters, more grandparents. These people need to be called by new and respectful names. No one takes the place of anyone else. Boundaries are extended to allow more people into the family.

Daddy's Girl—Sexual Boundaries

Natural taboos against incest are strong in first-marriage families. Even so, many times these are violated and children are sexually abused by parents or siblings. For stepfamilies, the danger is even greater. Since blood ties do not exist between all members of the household, sexual attractions may flourish.

Special caution should be taken when stepsiblings are teens. Helpful family rules may include:

1. All family members are fully clothed in public parts of the house.

2. Bedroom and bathroom doors are closed when people are undressed.

3. Opposite-sex teens are not left unsupervised in the house.

4. Affection among stepfamily members should be expressed cautiously. Romantic expressions of love should be recognized as just that.

Walking on Water—Family Worship

After nearly 20 years of marriage, the couple sitting in my office were contemplating divorce. They called themselves Christians and were church members. I asked the husband, "Have you led your family in worship at home?" He shook his head no.

The scriptures tell us to "train a child in the way he should go" (Proverbs 22:6). Paul writes, "Fathers, do not exasperate your children; instead, bring them up in the training and instruction of the Lord" (Ephesians 6:4). The teaching received at church may not be enough to keep our families walking in step with Christ. It must be reinforced by family worship at home.

Stepfamilies can enjoy a bonding experience that draws them closer to each other during family worship. Here are three guidelines I suggest for family worship:

1. Keep it short. Finding time when all members can be present is a challenge (it might even qualify as a miracle). So use the time wisely.

2. Keep it simple. Read a scripture portion in modern English. Teach children the power and effectiveness of prayer. Hymns and choruses, poems, or short inspirational readings may enhance the experience.

3. Keep it interesting. Attention spans vary. Plan wor-

ship with this in mind. Rotate responsibility for portions of the worship experience among stepfamily members. Make God a comfortable resident of the family.

Stepfamilies suffer from lack of tradition. Members do not share a common history. Family worship helps create a common bond, the building of tradition.

Blest Be the Tie That Binds—Stepstrangers

After stepchildren become adults, their ties to stepparents may weaken. These adult "strangers" may not enjoy spending a lot of time together. If this is so, it may be better for the birth parent to visit the adult child alone. And that's OK. Stepfamilies are different from first-marriage families, and their members relate to each other differently. It is fine to allow the bonding cords to be looser.

Still, by following the suggestions we've discussed, Christian stepfamily members will be better able to keep in step with God's Spirit, as well as treat each other with respect.

Jack M. Barnell is a marriage counselor and an associate professor of psychology at MidAmerica Nazarene College, Olathe, Kans.

Chapter 13

When Jenny Comes Marching Home (Again)

by Harold Ivan Smith

Background Scripture: Luke 15:11-32; 1 Timothy 5:8

When Johnny Comes Marching Home Again" was a popular song when I was in elementary school because we got to shout "Hurrah! Hurrah!"

Well, Johnny—and Jenny—are marching home again, but some parents aren't exactly shouting with enthusiasm. That's because Johnny is towing a rented trailer. And he's planning on staying indefinitely.

He's part of an emerging group of undecided or uncommitted young adults, a generation of grown-ups still clinging to the parental purse strings.

And while their parents may be dreaming of an "empty nest" and buying a condominium, re-nesters are upsetting those plans.

"I started out with three kids at home," says one mother. "Now I'm down to four."

That's the new math: two children have moved out but one divorced daughter moved back with toddlers.

"How do I know if I can cope with the empty-nest syndrome when the kids keep moving back in?" asks a father whose daughter seems to go broke about once a year.

Family experts have written about bed-wetting, thumb-sucking, and acne, but few have written about the NQAs—Not Quite Adults. There are lots of them—about 16 million adult children living at home. That's 35 percent of those in their early 20s (age 22-24) and 14 percent of those in their *late* 20s (25-29).

A Modern Trend

It wasn't always so. Before the Great Depression, most children married young and left home promptly. Then during the Second World War, single sons went to war while daughters went to war industries or other city jobs, thus launching the single-adult movement.

By the 1960s most children moved out on their own as quickly as possible. The few who didn't attracted attention, and their parents were criticized for not shaking the nest. But between 1969 and 1980 the trend reversed, and the number of young-adult children living at home increased 25 percent. Some were enrolled at nearby colleges, while others were recovering from an early divorce. Still others simply didn't want to accept the responsibility of independence. For many families this became the Age of Postponement, stretching adolescence into the mid-20s.

It doesn't take an economist to figure out the advantages for the back-to-home crowd. Erma Bombeck once listed them: free (or subsidized) rent, free laundry service, free toiletries, security, love, unlimited storage facilities, financing and loans at generous interest rates, free TV and VCR, and a permanent address for mail.

After all, apartments can be lonely and expensive—especially when parents have bedrooms to spare. Some NQAs, of course, are saving money for admirable goals such as going back to college, making a down payment on a house, or even starting a business. But others re-nest simply to keep up a comfortable life-style.

And some come home for altogether different reasons; they want to mend relationships. Cheryl, 26, said, "I wasn't a Christian when I was a teenager, and those years were a nightmare for my folks. Now my mom is dying of cancer, and my dad needs me to help. . . . I suspect he needs me, period."

Day-to-Day Hazards

Whatever the motives, re-nesting has some built-in hazards. Here are four common tensions cited by Monica O'Kane in her book *Living with Adult Children.*

• **Space and territory**—leaving clothes, dirty dishes, books, personal items scattered throughout the home; closed doors; rejecting privacy; problems with entertaining; sharing bathrooms.

• **Time**—asking somebody to do something "now"; not enough time to complete chores; tying up the telephone; expecting meals on "my" schedule.

• **Possessions**—borrowing clothes, money, food, cars.

• **Sound**—disrupting or annoying volume on the stereo, television, or radio (or all three at once); late-night coming and going.

Tensions can be intensified by poor communication

and "emotional archaeology," or digging up the past. Big problems seldom ignite a family ruckus, but misunderstandings and small irritations can lead to resentment, nagging, and open hostility.

These are all the worse if one of the parents didn't agree with the initial decision to take in the NQA. It can be particularly complicated when a stepparent is involved. One father tells of pacing the hallway between the slammed door of his second wife and the slammed door of his daughter—torn between two women he loves.

Moreover, parents and adult children must find new ways of relating. "Because I said so" or "This is my house and I make the rules" won't lead to harmony.

Sally faced that problem when she and her two children moved back home after her divorce. The first few weeks went well as she pulled herself together emotionally and paid some bills. Her mother helped with the children. But problems began when Sally started dating.

"Here I am stuck at home with her kids while she's out gallivanting," her mother fumed.

Sally's father confronted her with biblical objections to remarriage, and mealtimes became theological battlefields with nuances of Greek verbs tossed around like hand grenades. The family relationship was spoiled, and she eventually moved out with deeper wounds.

What does it take to be a parent, like the father in Jesus' parable of the prodigal son, who welcomes the returning young adult with open arms and a jubilant attitude? When we read that story in Luke 15, we sense excitement, restitution, and love instead of anger or tension.

There are thousands of sons and daughters today living in exile, perhaps still in the same zip code, but afraid to go home. They fear the spoken or unspoken "I told you sos," the smug look of victory on a parent's face. But they yearn for a haven in a ruthless world.

A Few Guidelines

If such a homecoming is to work, attitudes must be right. At the same time, some practical guidelines must be considered to help the new relationships blossom. Here are several:

1. Negotiate a reasonable (not just token) amount for room/board/laundry/telephone/heat/electricity. Ann Lander's suggestion of 25 percent of take-home pay is not far off.

2. Bear in mind that everyone has a right to privacy—parents as well as adult children.

3. Whoever makes a mess cleans it up.

4. Be specific about kitchen privileges, meal planning, "refrigerator raids."

5. Decide at the outset how long the arrangement will last. Set a time limit, if necessary.

6. Set specific times to pray together, talk over issues, and monitor the arrangement.

7. Expect re-nesters to respect your personal values, even if they disagree. It is, after all, your house. If they find your values cramp their single style, help them move out.

8. However, remember that all adults are entitled to their opinions.

The area of money requires special attention. I honestly believe parents should not walk around with open wallets, reaching for every restaurant bill or car repair. Adults need to pay their own way as much as possible, and everyone should be clear about the meaning of "Pay you back later."

Should you make loans? Far better to help your son or daughter get to know a nearby banker. If you do decide to loan money yourself, it's usually a good idea to put everything in writing: amount, terms, repayment schedule, cancellation privilege. This isn't being mean; this prevents future misunderstanding, resentment, and charges of favoritism by other siblings. (Plus, what happens if you or your spouse suddenly die? Your executor will need to know what's what.)

Obviously, keep your spouse informed about any loans or gifts. Some offspring are adept at working both sides of the street.

The nest you offer your son or daughter should be comfortable but not too cozy. That, admittedly, is a tough balancing act.

Robert Frost once said home is the place where, when you have to go there, they have to take you in. That holds true even for parents who have hoped to raise a highly motivated mover and shaker but find themselves with a confused young adult on their doorstep. In such situations Paul's exhortation to provide for the needs of one's immediate family takes on new meaning (1 Timothy 5:8).

Yes, it's stressful at times. Frustrations can creep in, and parents can feel like giving up on their child. But the words of Galatians 6:9 are a valuable watchword: "Let us not become weary in doing good, for at the proper time we will reap a harvest if we do not give up."

The last chapter has not yet been written.

Harold Ivan Smith is founder of Tear Catchers, a Kansas City, Mo., ministry to single adults. He is the author of several books, including *You and Your Parents: Strategies for Building an Adult Relationship.*